Learning English Made Simple

Sheila Henderson

Edited and prepared for publication by The Stonesong Press, Inc.

A Made Simple Book
Broadway Books
New York

A previous edition of this book was originally published in 1991 by Doubleday, a division of Random House, Inc. It is here reprinted by arrangement with Doubleday.

For information, address: Broadway Books, a division of Random House, Inc., 1540 Broadway, New York, NY 10036.

Edited and prepared for publication by The Stonesong Press
Managing Editor: Sheree Bykofsky
Design: Blackbirch Graphics, Inc.

PRINTED IN THE UNITED STATES OF AMERICA

Visit our website at www.broadwaybooks.com

First Broadway Books trade paperback edition published 2002.

The Library of Congress Cataloging-in-Publication Data
has cataloged the Doubleday edition as:
Henderson, Sheila, 1950–
Learning English made simple/Sheila Henderson.—1st ed. in the U.S.A.

A MADE SIMPLE BOOK—T.p. verso.
1. English language—Textbooks for foreign speakers.
I. Title
PE1128.H429 1990
428.3' 421—dc20 90-3123
ISBN 0-385-26794-0 CIP

19 18 17 16 15 14 13 12 11 10

CONTENTS

Introduction: **Read This First!** *6*

PART ONE

Chapter 1· **Finding a Place to Live/Asking** *10*

Chapter 2: **Getting a Job/Telling** *21*

Chapter 3: **Banking/Giving Instructions** *30*

Chapter 4: **Shopping/Comparing** *40*

Chapter 5: **Sending Letters and Packages/Requesting** *48*

Chapter 6: **Eating in a Restaurant/Recommending** *56*

Chapter 7: **Talking on the Telephone/Apologizing** *65*

Chapter 8: **Getting Around Town/Suggesting** *72*

Chapter 9: **Visiting a Doctor/Describing** *80*

Chapter 10: **Talking to Your Landlord/Complaining** *88*

Chapter 11: **Talking to Your Boss and Co-workers/Problem Solving** *95*

Chapter 12: **Going to School/Disagreeing** *105*

Chapter 13: **Buying a Car or Other Major Item/Advising** *115*

Chapter 14: **Going to a Social Event/Introducing** *123*

Chapter 15: **Going on a Trip/Planning** *130*

Chapter 16: **Using Government and Community Services/Insisting** *139*

PART TWO

Chapter 17: **Using Words That Name People, Places, and Things** *148*

Chapter 18: **Using Words That Tell the Action** *154*

Chapter 19: **Using Words That Describe** *161*

Chapter 20: **Using Words That Connect** *165*

Chapter 21: **Using Different Kinds of Sentences** *169*

APPENDIX A: Pronunciation Guidelines *174*

APPENDIX B: Numbers and Measurements *180*

ANSWER KEY: Exercise Answer Key *186*

Read This First!

Who should use this book?

Is this book for you? To find out, answer these two questions:

• *Are you new to this country?* You may have been here for only a few days, weeks, or months. Perhaps you are joining your family or friends. Maybe you and your family have come together. Or perhaps you have come alone.

• *Do you feel you need to learn better English to live easily here?* You may have studied English in school, or perhaps you learned by listening to English-language programs and reading English-language materials. You might even have had a chance to talk to English speakers. Now you must learn to speak and understand this new language better than ever before.

If you answered both of these questions with "yes," then you are one of the people *Learning English Made Simple* was written for:

- People who are newcomers to this country... who want to learn to live successfully in an English-speaking society.
- People who can read and speak simple English... who want to learn to communicate better in this language.

What is this book meant to do?

The purpose of *Learning English Made Simple* is to help you speak and understand English in the many typical situations that you will face while you live in this country. It is also meant to be a "survival manual" for you—to teach you how things are done here. As the book teaches you about this society, it will also teach you how to correctly use different kinds of English words and sentences. Although the book is meant to improve your speaking skills, it will probably improve your reading skills, too. However, this book is *not* meant to help you learn to write in English.

How is this book organized?

Learning English Made Simple has two main parts. Part One has sixteen chapters that talk about how to do many different things in this country. You may need to find a place to live or a job. You may need to know how to get around town or how to use the telephone. Maybe you need to go shopping. All of these situations are covered in this part of the book.

- Each chapter gives you a long list of *Useful Words* relating to the subject or situation that it covers.
- Then it tells you important facts or gives you helpful instructions about the subject or situation.
- Next there are several *Sample Conversations* showing people like you speaking correctly in those situations.
- Finally, each chapter ends with a section called *Language Skills* that teaches you ways to correctly use words and sentences that you might need to use in those situations. There are lots of examples and exercises to help you learn.

Part Two includes five chapters on language skills. These chapters teach you basic rules about English grammar. If you want to improve your understanding of how English works, you can study this part of the book by itself. Or you can use it as a special resource to help you review things that are taught in Part One.

This book includes two special sections at the end. One covers some basic information about how to pronounce English words. The other covers numbers and measurements. Refer to these sections whenever you are confused about pronunciation or measurements.

How to use this book

To get the greatest benefit from this book, you must actively participate with it. Don't just sit and read, skipping over words you don't know and ignoring the exercises. Instead, push yourself to learn as much as you can.

- If you do not already own a good two-language dictionary, buy one! Always keep your dictionary nearby as you read this book. Whenever you come across a word you don't understand, look in your dictionary for the meaning in your native language. You will certainly learn more from this book if you do—and you will learn more English words, too.
- Also, do the language skills exercises in each chapter. And especially be sure to do the *Practices* at the end of each chapter. Find a friend—someone who speaks English better than you—to practice with. (A native English speaker is the best.) If you want to improve your speaking and understanding of English, *nothing works as well as practicing with other people.*
- Use this book like a dictionary or a map. When you hear or read something that you don't understand, see if you can find information about it here. The chapters in Part Two and the sections at the end of the book on pronunciation and numbers will be especially useful to you in this way.

As you learn more about this country, its customs and its language, we hope that you will begin to feel "at home" here. From the very beginning, this country has been home to people from many other countries. Whether you plan to stay here and become a citizen—or to return to your native country sometime in the future—remember that you are more than just a "guest" here. You are part of the family. Welcome.

PART ONE

CHAPTER ONE

Finding a Place to Live/Asking

Finding a place to live is one of the first things you need to do when you come to a new country. So many things may seem strange to you. You may not feel comfortable without a place to call "home," a place where you feel safe and comfortable. To find a home, you must follow these three steps:

- Decide:
  1. How much space you need.
  2. How much you can pay.
  3. The part of town you want to live in.
- Visit several places.
- Sign a lease or rental agreement.

Decision #1: How much space do you need?

Homes are usually described by the number of bedrooms. Most have two, three, or four. Most homes also have a living room, a kitchen, one or more bathrooms, and perhaps a dining room or a den.

How many bedrooms you will need depends on how many people are in your household. Some towns have laws about how many people can live in a home. Landlords can also limit the number of people who live in their rental homes.

Answer the following questions to help you decide how large your home needs to be:

1. How many bedrooms would you need if you had one for each couple and one for each child in your household? Perhaps you think you can't afford so many, but you may be surprised.
2. How many bedrooms do you need if each couple has a bedroom and two or three children share each of the other bedrooms? Look for homes that have at least this many bedrooms.

Decision #2: How much can you pay?

Here's how to find out how much you can afford for rent each month:

Add up the money each person in your household makes each month. This is your total monthly household income. Next, divide your total income by 3. The answer is about the amount of money you should pay each month to rent your home. You might spend a little more or a little less.

USEFUL WORDS

Action words	Naming words	Describing words
to look for, to seek (a home)	apartment	furnished
to make a deposit	complex	unfurnished
to pay (the deposit, the rent)	duplex	carpeted
to lease, to rent	town house	central
to move in	condominium	air-conditioned
to give notice	house	fenced
to provide	heater, furnace	efficient, efficiency
to fix, to repair	air conditioner	private, privacy
to spray (for bugs)	appliances	accessible
to clean (the apartment, the duplex, the house)	refrigerator	convenient
to paint (the apartment, the duplex, the house)	stove	electric
to maintain (the apartment, the duplex, the house)	microwave	gas
	dishwasher	expensive
	washer/dryer	cheap, inexpensive
	connections, hookups	large, spacious
	fan, ceiling fan	small, cozy
	maintenance	
	sewer, septic tank	
	deposit	
	lease, lease agreement	
	(give) notice	
	landlord, manager	
	resident, tenant	
	bugs, pests	
	location	
	rent payment	
	swimming pool	
	fireplace	
	security	
	laundry room	
	garage, carport	
	household	

Decision #3: In what part of town do you want to live?

Many cities have companies that will help you find a home to rent. Look in the newspaper in the section called Classified Advertisements for "Rental Services." In the yellow pages of the telephone book, look under "Apartment Rental Information and Services" or "Real Estate Rental Service." These services usually charge a fee if they find a home for you.

You can also look for a home on your own:

1. Get a map of the area you live in. You can buy an inexpensive map at a grocery store, gas station, or bookstore. Mark the map with dots to

show where everyone in the household works or goes to school. If you depend on the bus to get you to work, get a bus schedule with a map. (You can usually find one at the public library.) Draw in the bus lines on your map.

2. Look in the Classified Advertisements in your Sunday newspaper for a city map. Most city newspapers publish a map that divides the city into parts. Draw the dividing lines on your map.

3. Now you're ready to choose the part of the city you want to live in. You'll probably want to live near the bus or highway that takes you to work. Can you find a home close to a school so the children can walk to school?

4. Look in the newspaper Classified Advertisements under "For Rent" or "Rentals." Read all the rental ads in the part of town you want to live in. Circle ads that:

- Have the right number of bedrooms.
- Are the right price.

Sometimes the information you need is not in the ad. If not, then call the telephone number given in the ad. Ask the person who answers the telephone the questions you have.

Now you are ready to visit some rental homes.

> VERY LARGE. All bills paid. Unfurnished efficiency/1br $292, 2-1½ $350, walking distance from major shopping and schools. On bus line. Swimming pool, laundry room. No pets. Oak Hill Apartments, 111 Seasons Road. 555-6231. EQUAL OPPORTUNITY HOUSING

Look at the example of a rental ad. Here's what it means:

VERY LARGE. The first part of an ad tries to get you interested in the place. In this ad, they want you to know that the rental home is large. When you see it, you may or may not agree.

All bills paid. Your monthly rent includes the cost of your utilities. You won't have to worry about your expenses going up and down each month. But your rent payment will probably be higher than it would be if you had to pay your utility bills yourself.

Unfurnished. This means you must have your own furniture.

Efficiency/1br $295. Efficiency means an efficiency apartment. Most efficiency apartments

HOW TO READ A RENTAL AD

Rental ads use abbreviations to shorten common words. Here are some abbreviations and key words you will find in advertisements:

br: bedroom.
lr: living room.
k: kitchen.
sqft: square feet.
WD or ***W/D:*** clothes washer/dryer.
CACH: central air conditioning and central heating.
all appliances: dishwasher, refrigerator, and stove are included; may also include microwave oven; usually does not include a clothes washer and dryer.
2-2: two bedrooms, two bathrooms.
2-1½: two bedrooms, one and one-half baths (a half bath has a toilet and sink but no bathtub or shower).
all bills paid: all utility costs are paid as part of the monthly rent (utilities include gas or electricity, water, and sewer, but not telephone).
furnished: furniture is included.

are one big room with a kitchen area on one side and space for a bed, usually with a separate bathroom. *1br* means one bedroom. A one-bedroom apartment has a separate bedroom and may have a separate kitchen. The ad says an efficiency apartment and a one-bedroom apartment each cost $295 a month.

2-1½ $350. These numbers mean that an apartment with two bedrooms and one and one-half bathrooms will cost $350 a month.

Walking distance from major shopping and schools. On bus line. This section of the ads tells you that this apartment is convenient.

Swimming pool, laundry room. This tells you that the ad is probably for an apartment complex. The apartment complex has its own swimming pool and laundry room for the people who live there.

No pets. Some landlords do not allow pets. If you have a dog or a cat, you will need to check to see if the place you want to rent will allow pets. You may have to give your landlord extra money as a "pet deposit" before you can move in. If your pet does no damage to the walls or carpets, you will get the pet deposit back when you move out. However, if your pet does damage something, you will not get your deposit back.

Oak Hill Apartments. This is the name of the apartment complex.

111 Seasons Road. This is the address of the apartment complex. You can drive by to see it.

555-6231. This is the telephone number of the complex. Call this number to ask questions about the apartments in the ad.

EQUAL OPPORTUNITY HOUSING. This means that the landlord does not discriminate against people for their race, creed, color, sex, or national origin.

Visit several places

Before you start your visits, remember two things:

1. Always visit several homes before you make a decision. The first place you see may be nice. But the next one you see may be even nicer.

2. Never let anyone force you to make a decision too quickly. Sometimes the people trying to rent to you will say things like "This is the last one" or "It will be gone tomorrow." Don't listen. They're just trying to get you to rent from them. Take all the time you need to decide where to live.

Prepare for your visits. Get a small notebook to take with you. At the top of each page, tape one rental ad that you have cut out of the newspaper. Call each place ahead of time to schedule a time to visit. Be sure you look clean and neat, and leave plenty of time between visits so you won't be late. But if you *are* going to be late for a visit, call to let the person know.

During your visit, you will be shown the rental home. In your notebook, find the page where you pasted the ad for the home you are visiting. As you walk around, write notes about what you see. Here are some questions to ask and some things to make notes about:

- *Is the home clean?* There should be no garbage, no spots on the walls. The floors and carpets should be clean. Nothing should be left by the person who lived there before. Ask if the walls have recently been painted. Many rental homes are painted before each new resident moves in. Look in the oven and refrigerator to see whether they are clean. The home should be clean and nothing should be broken.
- *Is the home free of bugs?* You should not see roaches, ants, spiders, or other creatures in the home. Ask if the landlord sprays for bugs. He should spray before you move in.
- *Is the home safe?* Are stairs safe to walk on? If there is a balcony, is the railing strong? Does the home have smoke alarms? Notice the locks on the doors. Do they look like they work well?
- *What are the rooms like?* Write down your comments. For instance, you might write "small kitchen" or "good light in the living room."
- *What is the outside like?* Is the area clean? Is the yard mowed? Are the trees well taken care of? If there is a pool, is it clean?
- *What are the other residents like?* The people you see will be your neighbors if you move in. Do you think you would like to live near them?
- *What are the costs to move in?* How much money will you have to pay as a deposit? (A deposit is money you must pay the landlord when you move in. It is often one month's rent.

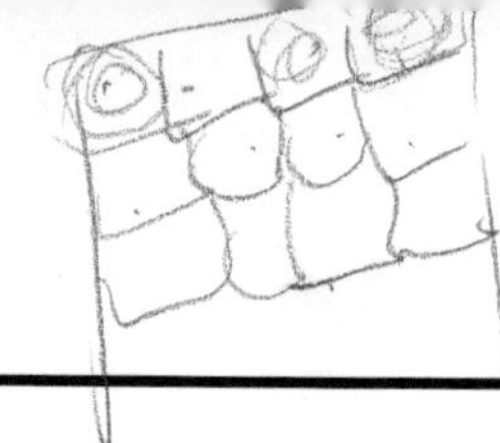

NAMES OF HOMES

Apartment. An apartment is a room or group of rooms to live in. Some apartments are a part of an old house. Most apartments are grouped together into apartment complexes. An apartment complex may have a swimming pool, a party room, and a laundry room for the people who live there. An apartment complex is usually owned by a company that has a manager to take care of all the apartments.

Condominium. A condominium is usually called a "condo." Condos are similar to apartments, except that condos are owned by individual owners. A condominium complex is run by an organization made up of all the individual owners. Like apartment complexes, condos often have extras, like swimming pools.

Duplex. A duplex is a building that has two living spaces—either side by side or one above the other. There are also triplexes with three living spaces and quadriplexes with four living spaces.

Town house. A town house is one of several houses in a row that share common walls. You often find five or ten town houses together. Town houses are usually larger than apartments and condos.

House. A house is a building that stands alone. Houses are usually larger and cost more than apartments, condos, duplexes, and town houses. They often have garages.

Home. A home is where you live. Your home may be an apartment, a condominium, a duplex, a town house, or a house.

If you move out before your lease ends or if you damage the apartment, the landlord will keep your deposit. Otherwise you will get it back when you move out.) Is there an extra deposit if you have a pet? How much is the rent payment and when is it due? When can you move in?

When you're finished, thank the person who showed you around and say that you will call later if you want to rent the home. Go to your other appointments until you have seen several places. You may have to look at twenty or more homes before you find the right one. You also may want to go back and visit a home a second time. If you have not found a place you want to live in, keep reading the ads in the newspaper and looking around.

Sign a lease or rental agreement

Once you've decided on the place you want to live, you must sign a lease or rental agreement. This is a legal piece of paper that says you agree to pay a certain amount of money to rent a certain home for a certain amount of time. The paper also lists any deposits you must make and other responsibilities that you and the landlord have. Most agreements are for 6 to 12 months. That means you are responsible for paying the rent for that long and cannot move out sooner than that without losing your deposit. As the end of your lease comes up, you must give notice 30 days before you can move out. If you want to stay in the home, you may sign a new lease for another 6 to 12 months.

To sign the rental agreement, call for an appointment with the person you talked to the first time. Say that you are interested in renting the home. The details of the rental agreement will be reviewed before you sign. Be sure you know what it says. Sometimes the language is hard to understand. If you can't read it, get someone to explain it to you. After you sign, you will need to pay your deposits and maybe your first month's rent.

Just before you move in, you will be given a walk-through of your new home: you and the landlord will walk through the home together, looking for problems. You may see a stain on the carpet or a hole in the wall. Be sure they are written down on the walk-through form. Otherwise, when you move out, your landlord might think you did the damage. Ask for all repairs to be made before you move in. Then you will be given a key and told the first day you can move in. (Chapter 10 tells more about leases and your relationship with your landlord.)

CALLING FOR INFORMATION: A SAMPLE CONVERSATION

Laura Chen is reading ads for apartments. She and her husband, Ping, need a two-bedroom apartment for themselves and their four-year-old daughter. Laura sees an ad for an apartment, but the ad does not tell how many bedrooms are in the home or how much it costs. Laura finds the telephone number in the ad and calls.

A voice on the telephone: Hello.
Laura: Hello. My name is Laura Chen. Are you with the Blackstone Apartments?
Voice: Yes. My name is David. How can I help you?
Laura: I saw an ad for an apartment in yesterday's newspaper. How many bedrooms does the apartment have?
David: We have several apartments for rent. How many bedrooms do you need?
Laura: I am looking for a two-bedroom apartment.
David: We have several two-bedroom apartments available at different prices.
Laura: What is the difference between the apartments?
David: Well, we are renting one on the ground floor for $400 a month. It is sunny and bright, and rose bushes grow around the patio. We are painting it now and the maintenance man is putting a ceiling fan in the living room and bedrooms. We are also painting a two-bedroom apartment on the third floor. It will rent for $375 a month. It doesn't have ceiling fans, but it has a beautiful view from the balcony. Also, a two-bedroom apartment on the second floor will be available in two weeks for $325 a month. It also has a balcony.
Laura: What is the view from the balcony?
David: The balcony faces the swimming pool.
Laura: When will the other two apartments be ready?
David: They are available now.
Laura: Thank you. I'd like to tell my husband about these apartments. I will let you know if we decide to visit.
David: Thanks for calling. Call again if you need more information.

VISITING A HOME: A SAMPLE CONVERSATION

Laura and Ping found the location of the Blackstone Apartments on their map. They decided to visit because the apartments were only one block from the bus Ping took to work. He called and made an appointment.

Now Laura and Ping are arriving at the apartments. When they walk into the manager's office, they see a man sitting at a desk.

Man: Hello. Can I help you?
Ping: Hello. I am Ping Chen. This is my wife, Laura. I talked with David last night. He said we could look at some two-bedroom apartments this evening.
Man: I am David Evans. I'm glad you could make it.
Ping: Thank you.
David: If you'll follow me, I'll show you the apartments. You can see that several people are swimming. Our pool is very popular with the residents.
Laura: How often do you clean the pool?
David: Currently, a pool maintenance company cleans the pool once a week.
Laura: Where is the laundry room?
David: It's over there, on the other side of the pool. We provide eight washers and four dryers.
Ping: The gardens around this complex are beautiful. Who takes care of the grounds? Do you have a gardener?
David: No. We have two maintenance men. They keep the pool area clean, take care of the grounds, and do most of the repairs. Here we are on the third floor. This apartment became available only recently.
Ping: I see the painters are still working. When will the apartment be ready?
David: The painters say they will finish today. The carpet is being replaced tomorrow. The apartment will be ready on Thursday. When did you want to move in?
Ping: We hope to find a place soon. We are staying with relatives until we find our own place.
David: How many people will be living in the apartment?
Laura: Just us and our four-year-old daughter.

David: Do you have any pets?
Ping: No, but we are thinking of getting a kitten for our daughter. What is your rule about pets?
David: We allow one or two pets, but we are starting a new pet deposit of $200. The people who were living in this apartment had a dog that tore up the carpet. That is why we are replacing it. If your pet ruins the apartment walls or carpets, we will keep your pet deposit.
Ping: Who takes care of bug control here?
David: We do. A company will spray this apartment before anyone moves in.

David shows Laura and Ping the other two-bedroom apartments. Laura makes notes about each one. Now they are ready to leave.

Ping: Thank you for showing us these apartments. They are very nice. We'll call you later if we decide on one.
David: Thanks for coming by. Call me anytime.

LANGUAGE SKILLS

When you are looking for a place to live, you must ***ask*** many ***questions*** about the rental homes you are interested in so you can choose a good home for yourself and your family.

In this chapter, you will learn two important language skills for asking questions:

- How to use asking words to find out new facts.
- How to use action words to talk about the present.

Using Asking Sentences

Asking sentences are called *questions*. Questions begin in two ways: With an *action word* or *helping word* (*Will* they paint the apartment?) or with an *asking word* (*When* will they paint the apartment?).

- Questions that begin with an action word or helping word can be answered with "yes" or "no." (*Will* they paint the apartment? *Yes*.)
- Questions that begin with an asking word must be answered with a new fact. (*When* will they paint the apartment? *Next Tuesday*.)

In this chapter, you will study how to use *asking words*. These are the asking words you use to ask questions:

Asking words	***Examples***
• who	*Who* is the manager?
• when	*When* is the rent due?
• where	*Where* is the laundry room?
• why	*Why* are you replacing the carpet?
• what	*What* time can we come see the apartment?
• how	*How* often do you spray for bugs?
• which	*Which* apartment is available first?

To form an asking sentence:

- Begin a question with one of these asking words: **who, when, where, why, what, how,** or **which**.
- Follow the asking word with an *action word*, a *helping word*, or a *naming word*.
  - ***Action words and helping words:*** Some asking words can *only* be followed by certain action words or helping words. Those words are **who, when, where,** and **why**. Here are the action words and helping words that can follow these asking words:

Action words you can use	***Examples***
to be: am, is, are, was, were	Why *are* the windows open?
to do: do, does, did	How *does* the fire alarm work?
to have: have, has, had	Who *has* the door key?

Helping words you can use	***Examples***
will, would	When *will* the tenants move out?
must, should	What *should* I do about the mailbox?
can, could	Where *can* I store my bicycle?

Who is the only asking word that can *sometimes* be followed by *different* action words. Here are some examples:

Who *wants* to visit the duplex?
Who *cleans* the swimming pool?
Who *lives* next door?

• ***Naming words:*** **What** and **which** are the asking words that *sometimes* can be followed by naming words. Here are some examples:

Naming words

What *color* is the stove?	What *kind* of stove is it?
Which *house* has a nicer yard?	Which *yard* is bigger?

• ***Describing words:*** **How** is the asking word that *usually* must be followed by a describing word. Here are some examples:

Describing words

How *expensive* is the rent?	How *long* will it take to move?
How *soon* can we move in?	How *big* are the closets?

TO LEARN MORE ABOUT ASKING SENTENCES, STUDY CHAPTER 21.

Exercise 1.1

Here are some sentences about looking for a place to live. Each sentence is the *answer* to a question. In the space after each sentence, write a *question* to go with the answer. Begin your question with the asking word that is written before the space. The first question has been done for you. (The answer key is on page 186.)

1. Ping and Laura need a two-bedroom apartment. **How** many bedrooms do Ping and Laura need in their apartment ______________________?
2. The town house will be available in two weeks. **When** ______________________ ______________________?
3. The kitchen has a refrigerator, a stove, and a microwave. **What** ______________________ ______________________?
4. The house with the large living room and the garage is most expensive. **Which** ______________________ ______________________?
5. Juana will drive to work on Highway 10. **How** ______________________ ______________________?
6. The landlord wants a pet deposit because dogs have torn the rug. **Why** ______________________ ______________________?

7. We will give you a key when you sign your lease. **When** ______________________________
____?

8. The washer and dryer connections are in the garage. **Where** ______________________________
____?

9. The residents must water and mow the yard. **Who** ______________________________
____?

10. We can use the parking space on the side. **Which** ______________________________
____?

Using Action Words

You can talk about things in the present in five ways:

- Something that is true *in general.*

  Examples: I *want* to find a new place to live.
  He *wants* to find a new place to live.
  They *want* to find a new place to live.

- Something that happens *often.*

  Examples: I *look* in the Classified Advertisements every Sunday.
  She *looks* in the Classified Advertisements every Sunday.
  We *look* in the Classified Advertisements every Sunday.

- Something that is happening *at this specific moment.*

  Examples: I *ask* about the apartment in the ad.
  We *ask* about the apartment in the ad.
  They *ask* about the apartment in the ad.

In each of these cases, here is how to form the action word:

I *look*	We *look*
You *look*	You *look*
He *looks*	They *look*
She *looks*	

- There is a second way to talk about something that is happening *at this specific moment.*

  Examples: I *am looking* at an interesting ad in the paper.
  She *is looking* at an interesting ad in the paper.
  They *are looking* at an interesting ad in the paper.

In this case, the action word is formed by using a helping word and adding **-ing** to the end of the action word:

I *am looking*	We *are looking*
You *are looking*	You *are looking*
He *is looking*	They *are looking*
She *is looking*	

- Something that has been hapening in the recent past and is still happening.

    Example: I *have been fixing* the heater all day.

To talk about something that has been happening in the recent past and is still happening, use the helping words **have been** or **has been** and add **-ed** to the end of the action word.

I *have been fixing*	We *have been fixing*
You *have been fixing*	You *have been fixing*
He *has been fixing*	You *have been fixing*
She *has been fixing*	

Note: **Am, is,** and **are** can also be action words when they are used before a *naming word* or a *describing word*. They are helping words when they are used before another *action word*.

Examples: We *are residents* in this complex.
(*residents* is a naming word)
We *are happy* about our new home.
(*happy* is a describing word)
We *are moving* into our new home.
(*moving* is an action word)

Form the action word like this:

I *am*	We *are*
You *are*	You *are*
He *is*	They *are*
She *is*	

TO LEARN MORE ABOUT ACTION WORDS, STUDY CHAPTER 18

Exercise 1.2

Here are some sentences from the conversation between the Chens and David Evans. After each sentence are two choices. Choose the one that describes the way the person is talking about the present. Put an "X" in the space beside your choice. The first sentence has been done for you. (The answer key is on page 186.)

1. I **am looking** for a two-bedroom apartment.
   _____ something that happens *often*
   _X__ something that is happening *at this specific moment*
2. Rose bushes **grow** around the patio.
   _____ something that is true *in general*
   _____ something that happens *often*
3. We **are painting** a two-bedroom apartment on the third floor.
   _____ something that is true *in general*
   _____ something that is happening *at this specific moment*
4. You can see that several people **are swimming**.
   _____ something that is happening *at this specific moment*
   _____ something that happens *often*
5. A pool maintenance company **cleans** the pool once a week.
   _____ something that is happening *at this specific moment*
   _____ something that happens *often*
6. We **provide** eight washers and four dryers.
   _____ something that is happening *at this specific moment*
   _____ something that is true *in general*

7. I see the painters **are** still **working**.
   _____ something that is happening *at this specific moment*
   _____ something that happens *often*
8. The painters **say** they will finish today.
   _____ something that is true *in general*
   _____ something that happens *often*
9. We **are thinking** of getting a kitten for our daughter.
   _____ something that happens *often*
   _____ something that is happening *at this specific moment*

Exercise 1.3

In this conversation, underline the action words that best tell the speaker's meaning. The first one has been done for you. (The answer key is on page 186.)

Aziz: Riad, we must talk about what kind of home we (1) **[are looking]** **[look]** for.

Riad: I (2) **[want] [am wanting]** to live in a house with three bedrooms and a big garage.

Aziz: A three-bedroom house is very expensive, Riad! We only (3) **[need] [are needing]** one bedroom to sleep in.

Riad: I am sewing a lot these days. I (4) **[am wanting] [want]** a room for my sewing machine and all my sewing things.

Aziz: Okay, one extra bedroom is a good idea. What is the third bedroom for?

Riad: It is for our family to stay in when they visit. Your mother (5) **[visits] [is visiting]** every year and (6) **[is staying] [stays]** for at least a month. Where can she sleep in a one-bedroom house?

Aziz: I (7) **[understand] [am understanding]** what you mean, but I (8) **[think] [am thinking]** we cannot afford such a big house. They are renting for $500 a month or even more!

Riad: Maybe we can look in an area that is inexpensive. In some areas away from the center of town, the houses (9) **[cost] [are costing]** less money.

Aziz: I (10) **[am driving] [drive]** thirty minutes to get to work already, Riad! You (11) **[are talking] [talk]** about adding fifteen or twenty more minutes to my drive. I think we must settle for only two bedrooms. The extra bedroom can be your sewing room when we do not have visitors. What are you doing?

Riad: I (12) **[am looking] [look]** for the newspaper. Let's see what is available.

Practice

Make up questions to find out about the place where your friend lives. Begin your questions with the seven asking words: *who, when, where, why, what, how,* and *which.*

Make up sentences that talk about the present. Talk about the place where you live and the things that you do there. Be sure to make up sentences that:

- Talk about something that is true in general.
- Talk about something that happens often.
- Talk about something that is happening at this specific moment.

CHAPTER TWO

Getting a Job/Telling

Many people come to this country because of the opportunities for work. Having a job means having money to take care of yourself and your family. To get a job, you must follow three steps:

- Look for a job.
- Apply for the job.
- Interview for the job.

Look for a job

You can look for a job four different ways.

• *Classified Advertisements*. Jobs are listed in the newspaper in a section called Classified Advertisements. The jobs are grouped together under headings for each type of work. For example, a job as a construction worker or a factory worker may be listed under "Industrial Trades." A job as an office worker may be listed under "Office/Clerical." A job as a waiter or a cook might be listed under "Clubs/Restaurants." A job as a babysitter or a housecleaner may be listed under "Domestic." Many other types of jobs—such as driving a truck or working a cash register—are listed under "General Help Wanted."

• *Government employment agency*. Many towns have a government office that helps people find jobs. Look in the telephone book to find the address of this office in your town. When you go to the office, you will fill out forms that ask about your school and work experience. Then someone will talk to you to find out what kind of work you can do.

• *Private employment agency*. Almost every town has companies that help people find jobs. Look in the yellow pages under "Employment Agencies" and call to make an appointment. When you go for your appointment, you will fill out forms that ask about your school and work experience—just like at the government employment agency. Then someone will interview you. If the company helps you find a job, either you or your new employer will have to pay a fee.

• *Job postings*. Large employers—like government agencies, colleges and universities, big companies—usually post job openings in their personnel offices. Some of these employers post their job openings on bulletin boards where you can see them. Others put them into large notebooks that you can look through. Look at the job postings at different places where you might want to work.

Apply for the job

After you find a job opening you are interested in, the next step is to apply for the job. To apply, you must go to the employer's office to fill out the application forms. Different companies use different application forms. But most application forms ask the same things:

- Name.
- Address.
- Telephone number.
- Date of birth.
- Place of birth.
- Social security or social insurance number.
- Names of schools you went to, the years you were there, and sometimes what you studied.
- Whether you were in the military service (Army, Navy, Marines, Air Force, Coast Guard, National Guard or Militia), the years you were there, and your rank.
- Names of places where you worked, the years you worked there, the type of work you did, and sometimes how much money you were paid.
- The names and telephone numbers of people who know you. These are called references.

A Classified Advertisement usually tells you how to apply for the job it advertises. Often it gives a telephone number for you to call to get more information. Sometimes it tells you the name of the person to talk to when you call. Some ads just give the company's address and tell you the times of day you can come to apply. Others list an address (like a post office box) where you can send a letter.

Employment agencies—both state agencies and private agencies—usually tell you how to apply for jobs they think you would like. The employment counselors tell you how to find the office where you can apply and the best times of day to go. Often they make an appointment for you to go and fill out your application and be interviewed.

TIPS ON APPLYING FOR A JOB

- Be well groomed. Wear nice clothes that are neat and clean.
- If you have an appointment, be on time or even a little early. Give yourself extra time to find the right building and office.
- Be prepared. Write down all the facts you will need for your application about your education and your jobs. Also write down the names, addresses, and telephone numbers of three or four references.

USEFUL WORDS

Action words	Naming words	Describing words
to look for, to seek (a job)	work, employment	full-time
to qualify, to be qualified	job, position	part-time
to apply, to make application	application, applicant	temporary
to interview, to be	advertisement, ad	available
interviewed	employment agency	immediately
to hire, to employ,	personnel	hardworking
to be employed	job posting	dependable
to earn, to make (money)	interview, interviewer	responsible
to be responsible for,	qualifications	experienced
to take care of	experience, background	qualified
to promote, to be promoted	education, training	skilled
to transfer, to be transferred	skills, abilities	
to quit, to resign,	trade, craft, profession	
to leave (a job)	manager, supervisor,	
to make, to build	foreman, boss	
to repair, to fix	advancement, promotion	
to operate, to run	references, recommendations	
(equipment, machinery)	salary, wages, hourly wage	
to file	benefits: insurance, sick leave	
to type	vacation, retirement plan	
to drive		
to cook, to prepare		
to serve, to wait tables		
to deliver		
to sell		
to clean		
to tend, to take care of,		
to watch		

Interview for the job

Some companies will interview you on the same day you fill out the job application. Other companies will study your application to decide if they want to interview you. They may take just a few days to decide. Or they may take as long as a month. If they decide to interview you, they will call to make an appointment with you. If you do not have a telephone, they may send you a letter asking you to call them. If they decide not to interview you, they will probably send you a letter to tell you.

An application form helps the company know what you have done in your life. But an interview helps them know what you are like. Are you honest and friendly? Do you follow instructions and work hard? Will you get along with the other workers and fit into the company? Someone must talk to you in person to find out if you would be a good employee.

An interview is also a way for you to find out more about the company and the job opening. does the company seem to care about the people that work there? Do the work areas look safe?

TIPS ON INTERVIEWING FOR A JOB

- Be well groomed. The people who interview you will judge you on how you look.
- Be on time. Even try to be a little early if you can. Give yourself extra time to find the right building and office.
- Try to relax. It's okay to be nervous, but try not to get too nervous. If you are very nervous, the interviewer may not be able to see what you are really like.
- Be prepared to answer questions. Here are some questions you might be asked:

  Which of your previous jobs was your favorite? Why?
  What work have you done that you did not like? Why?
  What would you like to be doing in one year? In five years?
  Describe your idea of the perfect job for you.
  Describe something you did at work that you are proud of.
  What are your strengths as a worker?
  What are your weaknesses as a worker?
- Be prepared to ask questions. Think of questions you want to ask about the company and the job opening. You can write the questions down so you won't forget to ask them. Here are some questions you might want to ask:

  When can I expect my first job review? (A job review is when your boss goes over your work and tells you what you are doing well and what you need to improve.)
  When can I expect my first pay raise?
  If I am a really good worker, what jobs could I be promoted into?
  Does this company have training or educational benefits for employees?
  Will there be times when I must work overtime?
  Will I have to buy any special clothes or equipment for this job?
- When the interview is over, show the interviewer how glad you are to be interviewed. Here are some things you could say:

  Thank you for seeing me.
  I enjoyed talking with you.
  I appreciate your taking the time to talk with me.
  I look forward to hearing from you.
- It is a common custom in this country to shake hands at the beginning and the ending of a meeting. Be ready to shake hands with your interviewer if he (or she) puts out his hand.

Are the wages and benefits good or bad? Does the person who will be your supervisor seem fair and honest? Is the job right for you? You can ask questions during your interview. You can also watch carefully and note what you see.

An interview can last only 15 or 20 minutes, or it can last more than an hour. At most companies, you will talk to someone who works in the personnel office. Sometimes you will talk to the person who will be your boss if you are hired. In very small businesses, you may talk to the top person—the one who runs the whole company.

APPLYING FOR A JOB: A SAMPLE CONVERSATION

Jorge Nuñez found an advertisement for a job opening in the Sunday newspaper. The ad was for a job at ADC, Inc., a company that fixes heating equipment in office buildings. The ad gave the address of the company and said to apply Monday through Friday between 8 A.M. and 5 P.M.

It is ten o'clock on Monday morning. Jorge has come in to fill out an application. The first person he sees is the company receptionist.

Receptionist: May I help you?
Jorge: I am here to apply for the job that was advertised in yesterday's newspaper.
Receptionist: You need to go to the personnel office. It's down this hall, the second door on the right.
Jorge: Thank you.

When Jorge goes into the personnel office, he sees a secretary at a desk facing the door.
Jorge: Excuse me. I want to apply for the job you advertised.
Secretary: Which one?
Jorge: Service technician.
Secretary: Oh yes. Here is an application and a pen. Be sure to fill out everything. Don't leave any blank spaces. You can sit at that table over there. When you're done, bring the application back to me.
Jorge: All right. Thank you.

After Jorge has finished filling out his application, he takes it back to the secretary.
Jorge: Here is my application.
Secretary: Okay. Let's see . . . yes, everything looks fine.
Jorge: When can I expect to hear something about this?
Secretary: We will be taking applications through Friday. Sometime next week they'll start calling for interviews.
Jorge: So I can expect to hear about an appointment for an interview sometime next week?
Secretary: Yes, that's right.
Jorge: Thank you very much. Goodbye.
Secretary: Bye now.

INTERVIEWING FOR A JOB: A SAMPLE CONVERSATION

Jorge Nuñez waited nearly two weeks to hear about an interview at ADC, Inc. Finally he got a telephone call from Mrs. Hendrix in the personnel office. Mrs. Hendrix asked Jorge to come in for an interview the following Thursday.

It is 3 P.M. on Thursday. Mrs. Hendrix comes into the waiting room and introduces herself to Jorge. They shake hands. Then she walks with him to her office and closes the door. When she sits down at her desk, she looks at Jorge's application form.
Mrs. Hendrix: I see from your application that you worked as a maintenance man for five years at a factory in Mexico. What kind of work did you do?
Jorge: The factory made bicycles. I fixed many different kinds of machine tools—milling machines, grinders, welders, and even painting equipment. I also fixed other things in the factory. And I have done some electrical work.
Mrs. Hendrix: Oh, that's good. What kind of electrical work did you do?
Jorge: Well, I rewired part of the building. We were getting bigger paint sprayers in the painting area, and the old wiring could not handle the extra load. And I also took care of the coolers and the heaters in the building.
Mrs. Hendrix: What kind of heating system was it? Our company works only with the large central heating systems.
Jorge: The front offices had central heating. But in the factory area there were only small space heaters. I worked on both kinds.

After Mrs. Hendrix finds out more about Jorge's work experience, she asks him some questions about his strengths and weaknesses as a worker.
Mrs. Hendrix: Well, your work experience sounds pretty good for the job we have open. Now tell me about the *best* job you've ever had. What was it like? Why was it your favorite?
Jorge: The best job? I guess my favorite job so far was when I worked for my father's roofing business. It was hard work, but the people on my job crew were great to work with. We really worked as a team. I enjoy working with people. I mean, working together with them, doing a job together. But in most of my jobs, I have worked alone.
Mrs. Hendrix: Tell me about a time when you did something especially well—something you feel proud of.

Jorge: When I was working at the bicycle factory, I once saved them a lot of money. An important machine broke down. A special part had broken and had to be replaced. But it would take three weeks to get the part! The foreman told me that a big order for bicycles had to be finished in only ten days. I studied the machine and figured out how to make the part myself, right in the factory. A few days later the manager asked me to come to his office. He gave me a bonus for helping them get the big order finished on time.
Mrs. Hendrix: That's great! No wonder you feel proud about that. Now, let me ask you another question. In all the jobs you've had, what was it that you *disliked* the most? It could have been the work itself, or it could have been something about the company or the people.
Jorge: That question is hard to answer. I don't think I've ever had a job that I really *disliked*. As I said before, I didn't like working alone so much at the bicycle factory. The job I had at the gas station was the same way. But it was worse, because I was stuck in one place doing the same thing all the time. I like to move around and do different things. I guess I mostly dislike work that is too much the same from day to day. I get bored.

Finally, Mrs. Hendrix describes the job opening to Jorge. She explains what a service technician does, how much money the job pays, and the benefits ADC employees get (such as sick leave and health insurance). When she is done, she asks Jorge if he has any questions.
Jorge: Yes, I have a few things I'd like to know about. First of all, does ADC have any educational benefits? Do you give employees training programs?
Mrs. Hendrix: Yes, we do. All service technicians get regular training in the new kinds of heating equipment that we work on. Sometimes we send one or two workers to big heating industry meetings to learn about new technology.
Jorge: What about training to become a supervisor or a manager?
Mrs. Hendrix: We don't have that as often as the technical training. But we do send people to supervisor training sometimes. Are you interested in becoming a supervisor?
Jorge: I have thought about it in the past. I was planning to take a business course in school before I decided to come to this country. As soon as I have a job, I may take a business course at the community college.
Mrs. Hendrix: Well, I will make a note on your application that you are interested in advancement. Only one or two supervisor positions open up each year. You might have to wait a few years before you get a chance.
Jorge: That's okay. I think anyone who becomes a supervisor should know the company really well.
Mrs. Hendrix: Do you have any other questions?
Jorge: No, I can't think of any right now.
Mrs. Hendrix: Then I guess we're finished with the interview. We expect to hire someone for this job within two weeks. You'll hear from us by the end of the week.
Jorge: Thank you for seeing me, Mrs. Hendrix. I enjoyed talking with you and I look forward to hearing from you about this job.

LANGUAGE SKILLS

When you are looking for a job, you must answer many questions. You must ***tell*** about yourself and your past work experiences. ***Telling*** sentences *describe* something—such as how to run a machine—or *inform* about something—such as what wages a company pays for a certain job. (See Chapter 21 to learn more about telling sentences.)

In this chapter, you will learn two important language skills for ***telling*** about yourself and others:

- How to use action words to tell about events in the past.

- How to use naming or describing words to tell about things that belong to you.

Using Action Words

You can talk about things that happened in the past in four ways.

- Something that happened and ended at a specific moment in the past.

Example: I *fixed* the heater last Wednesday.

To tell about something that happened and ended in the past, add **-ed** to the action word.

- Something that happened over a specific period of time.

Example: I *was fixing* the heater while he talked.

To tell about something that happened over a specific period of time, use the helping words **was** or **were** and add **-ing** to the action word.

I *was fixing*	We *were fixing*
You *were fixing*	You *were fixing*
He *was fixing*	They *were fixing*
She *was fixing*	

- Something that happened at an unspecific time or period of time.

Example: I *have fixed* heaters for years.

- Something that happened in the recent past and has ended.

Example: I *have fixed* the heater for you.

To talk about something that happened at an unspecific period of time, or something that happened in the recent past and has ended, use the helping words **have** or **has** and add **-ed** to the action word.

I *have fixed*	We *have fixed*
You *have fixed*	You *have fixed*
He *has fixed*	They *have fixed*
She *has fixed*	

TO LEARN MORE ABOUT ACTION WORDS, STUDY CHAPTER 18.

Exercise 2.1

Here are some sentences that Jorge said in the sample interview. In the space beside each sentence, write the letter that describes the way Jorge is telling about his past. The first sentence has been done for you. (The answer key is on page 186.)

E: Something that happened and *ended* at a specific moment in the past.

S: Something that happened over a *specific* period of time.

U: Something that happened at an *unspecific* time or period of time.

R: Something that happened in the *recent* past and has ended.

_E_ 1. I fixed many different kinds of machine tools at my last job.

___ 2. I rewired part of the building.

___ 3. And I have done some electrical work.

___ 4. I worked on both kinds.

___ 5. But in most of my jobs, I have worked alone.

___ 6. I was working at the bicycle factory.

___ 7. I have thought about it in the past.

___ 8. I was planning to take a business course in school.

___ 9. I enjoyed talking with you.

Exercise 2.2

In this conversation, underline the action words that best tell the speaker's meaning. The first one has been done for you. (The answer key is on page 187.)

Edward: Lim, what is your experience? Are you qualified to be a bank teller?

Lim: When I (1) **[<u>started</u>] [have started]** at the supermarket, I worked as a cashier. I did that for two years. Later on, they promoted me to office manager. I (2) **[cashed] [was cashing]** checks and (3) **[sold] [was selling]** money orders.

Edward: Do you have other experience with money?

Lim: I (4) **[have done] [was doing]** some bookkeeping. I (5) **[handled] [have handled]** the bills, checks, and other money records for the Speedy Car Parts store.

Edward: Tell me more about your job at Speedy Car Parts. What were your responsibilities?

Lim: Well, at the beginning I (6) **[was working] [have worked]** as assistant to the office manager. After a few months, I (7) **[was starting] [started]** to pay the bills at the end of the month. Then I (8) **[took] [was taking]** over adding up the money every day and balancing the bank records every month.

Edward: That sounds like good experience for being a bank teller. What is your education?

Lim: I (9) **[graduated] [have graduated]** from high school in 1984. Since then, I (10) **[have studied] [studied]** typing and other office skills. Last spring, I (11) **[completed] [was completing]** a class in American history.

Edward: Well, Lim, I think your qualifications to work as a teller in our bank are very good. We will be in touch with you soon.

Using Naming and Describing Words

When you talk about something that belongs to you, you must show that by using a special naming or describing word. Things can belong to you in four different ways:

- Something you *have*.

  Example: I have a job at a restaurant. *My* job doesn't pay much money. But at least the job is *mine*. That's what *my* boss says!

- Something you *make*.

  Example: I wrote a report on the project. I finished *my* report last week. The ideas in the report were *mine*.

- Something you *give* or *do*.

  Example: I ordered a new drill. They filled *my* order right away. The first order they filled was *mine*.

- Something that you *experienced*.

  Example: I drove to the warehouse in the company truck. *My* drive was a nice break from *my* regular work. I don't think Frank's drive was as nice as *mine*.

Note: **My** is a describing word. It comes before a naming word: That is *my* job. **Mine** is a naming word. It replaces another naming word: That is *mine*.

TO LEARN MORE ABOUT NAMING WORDS, STUDY CHAPTER 17.

Exercise 2.3

This is what Jorge told his friend Edward about his interview at ADC, Inc. The sentences don't sound right. They don't use any naming words that show belonging. To make the story sound right, you must change the sentences. The words that must be changed are in bold letters. Write the words that show belonging in the empty space. The first sentence has been done for you. (The answer key is on page 187.)

1. I went for **[the interview I had]** ____my interview____ at 3 P.M. on Thursday.
2. I was so afraid that **[the hands I have]** ____________________ were sweating!
3. Mrs. Hendrix looked at **[the application I made]** ____________________ and asked about **[the experience had]** ____________________.
4. I told her about **[the job I had]** ____________________ at the bicycle factory.
5. She wanted to know if the responsibility of fixing the heaters was **[my responsibility]**____________________.
6. She asked me to tell her about **[the favorite job I had]** ____________________.
7. I told her about working for **[the father I have]** ____________________ at his roofing company.
8. By this time, **[the fear I had]** ____________________ was gone.

Practice

Make up sentences that tell about things you did in the past. Be sure to make up sentences that:

- Tell about something that happened and ended at a specific moment in the past.
- Tell about something that happened over a specific period of time.
- Tell about something that happened at an unspecific time or period of time.
- Tell about something that happened in the recent past and has ended.

In your sentences, use *my* and *mine* to tell about things that:

- You had.
- You made.
- You gave or did.
- You experienced.

CHAPTER THREE

Banking/Giving Instructions

Some newcomers to this country pay for everything with cash. That was how they did it in their native countries. Here, however, most people use bank checks instead of cash. If you put your money in a bank, you will have less trouble paying your bills. Also, your money will be safer. If you want to use the services of a bank, here's how to:

- Choose a bank.
- Open your accounts.
- Take care of your checking account.
- Learn to use special bank services.

Choose a bank

How do you choose among the many banks that offer services? Here are three things you need to think about:

- *How close is it to your home or your job?* Your bank should be easy to get to. Notice banks you pass in your neighborhood or on your way to work. Take time to visit some of these banks.

- *How well are you treated by the bank employees?* Your bank should treat you with respect and work hard for you. Watch how the bank employees treat the customers who come in. Notice whether they seem interested in helping you get information.

- *What kinds of services does the bank offer, including the interest that it pays? What fees does it charge?* Your bank should make handling money easier for you without costing you much money. When you are visiting a bank, pick up some of the free written materials sitting on tables or desks. These materials will tell you about the bank and the services it offers. Banks can offer many different services and benefits to their customers. They can have branch banks, drive-in teller windows, banking by telephone, automatic teller machines (ATMs), credit cards (like Visa and MasterCard), many different ways to save or invest your money, low fees and high interest rates.

USEFUL WORDS

Action words	Naming words	Describing Words
to open (an account)	checking account	drive-in
to deposit, to make a deposit	savings account	joint (account)
to withdraw, to make a withdrawal	deposit slip	direct (deposit)
to write (a check)	withdrawal slip	monthly
to balance (the checkbook, the account)	check(s)	financial
to cash (a check)	checkbook	
to overdraw (the checking account), to bounce (a check)	balance, account balance	
to wire (money, funds)	teller, teller window	
to credit	cash	
to debit	overdraft	
to earn (interest), to pay (interest)	check register	
to endorse	signature	
	bank statement	
	credit	
	debit	
	collateral	
	money order	
	cashier's check	
	endorsement	
	NOW account	
	money market account	
	traveler's check	
	automatic teller machine (ATM)	
	transaction	
	safe-deposit box	
	interest	
	identification	
	branch bank	
	credit union	
	savings bank, savings and loan	
	service charge, fee	
	receipt	

After you have looked at several banks, choose the one that is best according to these three points: (1) Your ideal bank should be easy to use. (2) It should employ people who do their jobs well and treat customers well. (3) It should offer the services and benefits that you are most interested in.

Open your accounts

You will probably want to open two kinds of accounts at your bank:

- A checking account.
- A savings account.

KINDS OF BANKING COMPANIES

When you look around for a bank, you may find several different kinds of banking companies. Some of these companies offer the same kinds of services and benefits, but others do not. Here are the three kinds of banking companies:

Banks. These are the most common banking companies. They offer many different services: checking accounts, savings accounts, credit cards, and automatic teller machines. They also will lend you money for many different uses—for example, to buy a car or house, to pay for school tuition, or to pay off bills. Anyone can do business with a bank.

Savings and loans. These banking companies are very much like banks. They offer the same services and benefits. Anyone can do business with a savings and loan.

Credit unions. These banking companies are different from banks and savings and loans. They offer the same services and benefits, but they are not run in the same way. Credit unions are owned by the people who put their money in the credit union. Usually, credit unions are started for people who work for a certain kind of business. For example, only teachers can open an account at a teachers' credit union.

Open a checking account. To open your checking account, you must have some money to put into it. Some banks expect you to have several hundred dollars to open your account. You can open your account with a check (like a paycheck) or with cash.

To open an account, go into the bank and look for a desk with a sign that says "New Accounts." The New Accounts person will help you with the steps to open your account.

1. First, he or she will fill out a form with information about you:
   - Your name and address.
   - Your social security or social insurance number.
   - Your driver's license number.
   - Your employer's name and address.

If you don't have a driver's license, don't worry. You don't *need* a driver's license to open a checking account.

2. Next, he or she will ask you to choose the kind of account you want to open. Most banks have more than one kind of checking account. Some banks have four or five different kinds. With some accounts, you must pay the bank a service charge every month. With other accounts, the bank will pay *you* money, called interest. The kind of account you can choose depends on how much money you can keep in the account. When you have chosen the kind of account you want, the New Accounts person will assign you an *account number*.

3. The New Accounts person will then ask you to sign a signature card. The signature card must have the signature of everyone who will use the account. If the account is an individual account, then only you will sign the card and only you can write checks on the account. If the account is a joint account, then you and your husband, wife, or other relative (or friend) must both sign the card. That means that both of you must go to the bank to open the account. Even with a joint account, only one person needs to sign the checks, unless you tell the bank that two or three people must sign all checks.

4. Next, the New Accounts person will talk with you about the kinds of checks you can use with your account. You will probably get to choose the color of your checks and maybe even a special design. Your checks and deposit slips will have your name and address printed on them. Your account number will be printed at the bottom. You will have to pay a fee for these printed checks.

If you have never filled out a check, be sure to ask the New Accounts person to show you how.

5. You must start your account by depositing your money in it. The New Accounts person will fill out a deposit slip for you and take your check or cash to a teller. The teller will make the deposit and give you a receipt.

6. Once the paperwork is complete, including the deposit of your money, the New Accounts person will give you a temporary check-

book. After you leave the bank, you can write checks on your account, unless the New Accounts person has told you to wait until a certain day. In a week or so, your personal printed checks and deposit slips will come in the mail.

Open a savings account. Savings accounts are good for two reasons. First, you have money in case you need it. A good rule is to save enough money to pay for three months of your living expenses, just in case you get sick or have other problems. Second, you can make money by saving money. Banks, savings and loan companies, and credit unions all pay interest on money kept in savings accounts.

You can open an account at the bank where you have your checking account. Or you can look for another place to save your money—another bank, a savings and loan company, or a credit union. It is easier to do all your banking in one place. But you may want to put your money where it will earn the highest interest. See how much interest your bank is paying on savings accounts. Then check other places to find the best interest rate.

Opening a savings account is very similar to opening a checking account. The New Accounts person will do all the paperwork and take your deposit. Most banks expect you to deposit a certain amount of money to open your savings account. The amount is different at different banks. At some banks you will get a book in which the bank will record your savings. Whenever you deposit money in your savings account or withdraw money, the teller will record the amount in your book. Periodically—for example, every three months—the teller will also record your interest.

Take care of your checking account

Having a checking account makes your life easier in many ways. But it can be harder, too, if you don't take care of your checking account. Here are some rules for taking care of your account:

- Keep a record of all checks you write. Most checkbooks have a check register to record your checks. You must also be sure to record any ATM withdrawals you make. And don't forget to record your deposits as well.
- As you record each check or withdrawal, subtract the amount from your total checking account balance. As you record each deposit, add the amount to your balance. If you do this, you will always know how much money you have in your account. This is important. You don't want to write checks for money that isn't there.

When you don't have enough money in your account to cover a check, the bank will send the "bad" check back to the person or company whose name you have written on the check. The check "bounces." For example, if you write a bad check to pay your rent, the bank will send the check back to your landlord. At the same time, the bank will charge you a fee (called a penalty) for writing a bad check. The person or company that gets your check back will probably charge you a fee, too. Writing a bad check can be a very expensive mistake.

- Each month, you will get a statement from the bank. Use this statement to balance your checking account. The statement will tell you:
- How much you deposited that month.
- How much you wrote in checks.
- Any money that the bank charged your account, such as a service charge, or any interest earned if you have an interest-earning account.
- How much money is left in your account.

With most banks, you will also get back the checks that were paid from your account.

On the back of your bank statement is a form that will help you balance your checkbook. Follow the form. After you subtract all the bank's fees from your checkbook, your checkbook balance should be the same as the bank's. If it isn't, keep figuring until it is. Get help from the bank if you need it. Balancing your checkbook every month will help you know how much money you really have. And sometimes you'll find the bank has made a mistake.

If you subtract your checks from your account balance during the month and balance your checkbook at the end of the month, you should have no trouble taking care of your bank account.

HOW TO USE AN ATM MACHINE

Many banks offer their customers a special service called an ATM card. ATM means automatic teller machine. With an ATM card, you don't have to go to your bank to get money out of your account, to make deposits, or to find out how much money you have in your account. ATM machines are located in shopping centers, grocery stores, airports, and other handy places, including your bank (so you can do bank business even when the bank is closed). If you use an ATM card, your bank will charge your account for this service. They may charge a set amount every month, or they may charge a small fee each time you use the card.

An ATM machine is a computer. There are several different kinds of ATM machines, each with its own particular design. But all ATM machines have these features:

- A computer screen where the computer gives you instructions.
- A set of buttons to push when you give the computer instructions.
- A slot where you insert your ATM card.
- A slot where you can put money that you want to deposit.
- A place where the machine puts cash that you withdraw from your account.
- A slot where your receipt comes out when you are finished.

To use an ATM machine, you need your ATM card and a secret code number that the bank will give you. This is your *identification number* or *ID number.* Do not tell this number to anyone, even your friends. With the number and the card, *anyone* can take money from your account. Without the number, *no one* can use your card.

Three rules will help you use an ATM machine wisely:

1. Do not use an ATM machine to get large amounts of cash. If you want more than $100 or $200, go to your bank. Most people use the ATM machine to get less than $100.
2. Always remember to take your receipt (and, of course, your ATM card) from the ATM machine.
3. Always write down your ATM withdrawals in your check register, just like a regular check.

Learn to use special bank services

Banks offer many services you may need. Here are a few of these services you can use:

- *Loans.* Banks make loans to their customers for many different things. You can get a loan to buy a new car, to add on to your house, or to send your daughter to college. To get a loan, go to your bank and ask to see a loan officer. The loan officer will find out what you want the loan for. He or she will ask you questions and have you fill out forms that give information about you. The loan officer wants to find out if you can afford to make the loan payments every month. If he or she thinks that you can, you will probably get the loan. You may also have to give the bank something to protect them from losing the money they loaned you. This is called collateral. For example, when you get a loan to buy a new car, the bank is the official owner of the car until you have paid back the loan.

- *Cashier's checks and money orders.* These are good ways to send money to someone far away, perhaps someone in another country or in another state.

A *cashier's check* is made out to a *particular person.*

A *money order* is like cash, since it can be used by *anyone* who has it.

To get a cashier's check or money order, go to a teller at your bank. The teller will prepare the cashier's check or money order for you. You can give the teller the money in cash or you can ask him or her to withdraw it from your account. You must pay a small fee when you buy a cashier's check or money order.

- *Wire money.* If you often send money to another country, you may want to have it wired directly from your bank to a bank in that country. Go to a teller at your bank for this service. You must pay a fee for this service.

• *Traveler's checks*. If you are taking a trip, you can get traveler's checks. This is better than carrying large amounts of cash with you. If you lose traveler's checks, the finder cannot use them. And you can get new traveler's checks at no cost very easily. You must pay a small fee for traveler's checks.

• *Safe-deposit box*. A safe-deposit box is a good place to keep important papers and valuable things. Many people keep birth certificates, passports, or expensive jewelry in safe-deposit boxes. These boxes are secure in the bank, so your valuables will be safe from fire or theft. The bank will charge a yearly fee for your safe-deposit box.

OPENING A BANK ACCOUNT: A SAMPLE CONVERSATION

Nasir and Tama Kashem want to open a checking account. They have chosen the Fullerton Bank, which is near their new home. As they walk in, they see a desk with a sign that says "New Accounts." They walk up to the woman sitting at the desk.

Woman: Hello. Can I help you?

Nasir: Hello. We'd like to open a checking account.

Woman: You're at the right place. Please sit down. Are you new in town?

Tama: Yes. We moved into the River Plaza Apartments last month.

Woman: Well, we're glad you're here. My name is Vanessa Ruiz.

Nasir: I am Nasir Kashem and this is my wife, Tama.

Vanessa: We have several types of checking accounts, but they all require a $200 deposit to begin with. Can you deposit that much money today?

Nasir: Yes, that's fine.

Vanessa: This brochure tells about the different kinds of accounts here at the Fullerton Bank. The cheapest one costs only $3 a month, but you can only write ten checks. Most people prefer our personal checking account. Your service charge depends on how much money you keep in the account. We also have a special type of account if you expect to keep a balance of $1,500 or more.

Vanessa and the Kashems discuss the various accounts. They decide on the personal checking account. Vanessa types up several papers, which the Kashems sign. They give her Nasir's payroll check to deposit into the account. Vanessa gives them a temporary checkbook and tells them when their permanent checks will come in the mail.

Vanessa: Thank you for coming by. Let us know if we can be of further service to you. Here is some information you can read later about the many services we provide here at the Fullerton Bank.

Nasir: Thank you. We appreciate your help.

BANKING AT THE TELLER WINDOW: A SAMPLE CONVERSATION

Nasir and Tama Kashem have been banking at the Fullerton Bank for three months. Today, Tama has come in to take care of several things.

Teller: Hello. Can I help you?

Tama: Yes. Please deposit these two checks to my account.

Teller: I will be happy to, Mrs. Kashem. Have you endorsed each check on the back? Yes, I see you have. Okay, here's your receipt. Do you need anything else today?

Tama: Yes. Give me $200 in traveler's checks and $200 in cash.

Teller: Certainly. Do you want to write a check for the cash, or shall I debit your account?

Tama: Debit the account, please.

The teller takes some time to do the paperwork. Then she gives Tama her traveler's checks and cash.

Teller: Sign on this line for your cash, please. . . . Okay, Mrs. Kashem. Here is your money. And here are your traveler's checks. Sign each one on the top line, please. How do you want to pay for them?

Tama: Debit my account again.
Teller: All right. Sign this form right here, please. Will that be it for today?
Tama: No, one more thing. Give me a cashier's check for $20.
Teller: Whom should it be made out to?
Tama: Shazee Montgomery. She's my niece and next week is her sixteenth birthday.
Teller: Sixteen is such a special age, isn't it? How do you spell Shazee?
Tama: S-h-a-z-e-e.
Teller: It will be from you?
Tama: Me *and* my husband. Put Tama and Nasir Kashem. Debit that money from the savings account.
Teller: Okay. Here is your cashier's check. Send the top to Shazee and keep the copy for your records. I'll bet she'll be happy to get it.
Tama: I hope so. Kids that age do love to buy things.
Teller (laughing): That's certainly true! Is there anything else today, Mrs. Kashem?
Tama: No. Thank you for your help.

LANGUAGE SKILLS

When you open a bank account, you must make many decisions. Then you must ***give instructions*** to bank employees about the decisions you have made. In this chapter, you will learn three important language skills for ***giving instructions***.

- How to use action words to talk about the future.
- How to use sentences to tell people what to do.
- How to use naming words to talk about: close and far, one and more than one.

Using Action Words

There are two ways to talk about things that are going to happen in the future:

- You may use the word **will** + an action word.
  Example: I *will send* money to my granddaughter.

- You may use the words **will** + **be** + an action word + **-ing**.
  Example: I *will be sending* money to my granddaughter.

Both of these sentences mean the same thing. You can speak about the future in either way.

Sometimes we shorten the word **will** to the letters **'ll**. We add these letters to the word that comes before it.

Examples: She *will* like the present. She*'ll* like the present.
I *will* send her the present. I*'ll* send her the present.

When you talk about the future, the action word does not change whether you talk about yourself (*I* or *we*), someone or something else (*he, she,* or *it*), or several other people (*they*).

Examples: I *will see* you tomorrow.
He *will see* you tomorrow.
They *will see* you tomorrow.

We *will be seeing* you tomorrow.
She *will be seeing* you tomorrow.
They *will be seeing* you tomorrow.

TO LEARN MORE ABOUT ACTION WORDS, STUDY CHAPTER 18.

Exercise 3.1

The following sentences tell about something that is happening *now*. Change each sentence to tell about something that is going to happen *in the future*. The first sentence has been done for you. (The answer key is on page 187.)

1. Nasir and Tama **are opening** a checking account. ______Nasir and Tama will open a checking account.
2. They **live** at the River Plaza Apartments.____
____.
3. Nasir and Tama **have** an ATM number.____
____.
4. Nasir and Tama **put** $200 in their checking account._______________________________
____.
5. Vanessa **types** up several papers and the Kashems **sign** them.______________________
____.
6. Tama **deposits** two checks in her account.____
____.
7. Tama **wants** to write a check for cash.____
____.
8. Tama **has** her account debited for the traveler's checks.____________________________
____.
9. Nasir and Tama **open** a savings account.____
____.
10. Tama **goes** back to the bank alone.____
____.

Using Command Sentences

When you tell or ask someone to do something, you use a command sentence. This type of sentence usually begins with an action word. The person who is being told to do the action is not mentioned. The person understands that he or she is being asked or told to do something.

Examples: *Pick* up some brochures about the bank.
Deposit this check, please.
Hand me the checkbook.

To form a command sentence, drop the naming word at the beginning of the sentence.

Example: *You* order some new checks, please. Order some new checks, please.

Always use action words that talk about things that are happening in the *present*—not in the past or in the future.

TO LEARN MORE ABOUT COMMAND SENTENCES, STUDY CHAPTER 21.

Exercise 3.2

In this conversation, underline the action words that show a request or command. The first one has been done for you. (The answer key is on page 187.)

Nasir: (1) Tama, put some money in the checking account today.

Tama: (2) I put the checks in yesterday. Go to the ATM and get some cash to buy groceries.

Nasir: (3) I will get the money. On your way home tomorrow, please buy the groceries.

Tama: (4) When I finish with the shopping, I will stop at the post office to mail the bills. Give me the things to mail.

Nasir: (5) I have written out the checks. Please put them in the envelopes before you leave.

Tama: (6) Hand me my purse. I have stamps in it.

Nasir: (7) I have to go to the gas station. Give me the car keys from your purse.

Tama: (8) Here they are. While you are out, stop by the cleaners and pick up the shirts I took in yesterday. And let the dog in on your way out, okay?

Using Naming Words

Naming words can be actual names of things, like *account number* or *checkbook*. They can also be words that *stand for* names of things. **This, that, these,** and **those** are four words that stand for other words.

- **This** refers to one thing that is close to you.
- **These** refers to more than one thing that is close to you.
- **That** refers to something that is farther away from you.
- **Those** refers to more than one thing that is farther away from you.

Examples: The check register helps me manage my money.
This helps me manage my money.
The balance is correct.
That is correct.
The checkbooks are new.
These are new.
The accounts balance.
Those balance.

You may also use the words **this, that, these,** and **those** along with another naming word.

Examples: *This checkbook* is the one I want.
These accounts are the ones that balance.
That bank is the one I use.
Those receipts are important.

TO LEARN MORE ABOUT NAMING WORDS, STUDY CHAPTER 17.

Exercise 3.3

Underline the word that best completes the sentence. The first sentence has been done for you. (The answer key is on page 187.)

1. I found **[<u>these</u>] [this]** checkbooks at the bank.
2. Did you buy **[this] [those]** money order?
3. Is your savings in **[this] [these]** account or **[that] [those]** account?
4. Did Raúl withdraw money from **[this] [these]** automatic teller machine?
5. Stop at the bank tomorrow to deposit **[these] [that]** check.
6. **[That] [Those]** teller was very helpful today.
7. I got **[these] [this]** traveler's check at the bank today.
8. I paid **[that] [those]** overdraft last week.
9. I debited our checking account to buy **[these] [this]** traveler's checks.
10. She used the ATM card to get the money to buy **[these] [this]** money order.

Practice

Make up sentences that tell about something you will do in the future. Be sure to make up sentences that talk about the future using:

- *will*
- *will + be + –ing*
- and *'ll*

Also make up sentences that command or give instructions. Start these sentences with an action word.

In your sentences, use naming words that talk about things that are:

- Close.
- Far.
- One.
- More than one.

CHAPTER FOUR

Shopping/Comparing

There are many different kinds of stores in this country. They sell different products: some sell food, some sell clothes, others sell books or records. Some sell expensive things and others sell cheaper things. If you want to buy something, you need to know what kind of store to go to. Here is some helpful information about:

- Finding what you want to buy.
- Understanding how things are measured.
- Understanding how things are priced.
- Paying for your purchase.

Finding what you want to buy

Stores are usually organized to help people find what they want to buy. Things that are alike are put in the same area. Most stores use signs to help customers find the right area to look in.

• *Grocery stores, supermarkets, drugstores, and discount stores*. These stores usually are organized with long aisles. Each aisle has a sign hanging over it. The sign has names of products that are stocked on that aisle written on it. Sometimes these signs are numbered. If you ask a salesclerk where to find soup, she might tell you, "On aisle four." Here are some of the products that are placed together in these stores: produce, frozen foods, dairy products, meats, packaged foods, cleaning supplies, personal-care supplies, and other items, like toys, car-care products, and yard-care products.

• *Department stores*. Department stores—and many discount stores—are organized with the different clothing departments together in the same part of the store. There are departments for women, men, and children. Shoes, jewelry, belts and handbags, and cosmetics are in separate departments. Here are some other departments and what is in them: The housewares department has dishes, silverware, cooking utensils, and pots and pans. The hardware department has tools, paints, light fixtures, plumbing supplies, and other home improvement products. The appliance department has sewing machines, washers and dryers, refrig-

USEFUL WORDS

Action words	Naming words	Describing words
to shop, to go shopping	a shop, a store	refrigerated
to buy, to purchase	groceries	frozen
to pay (for)	loaf	canned
to charge	bottle, jar	fresh
to weigh	can	spoiled, rotten
to order	sack, bag	ripe
to examine	carton	dozen
to try on	box	half dozen
to alter	sale	clean
to compare	special	expensive
	shopping cart, shopping basket	inexpensive, cheap
	pair	for sale
	size	on sale
	customer	
	clerk, salesclerk	
	cost, price	
	produce	
	meat	
	dairy	
	mall, shopping mall	
	supermarket	
	department store	
	drugstore	
	bargain	
	delicatessen	
	pharmacy	
	price sticker, price tag	
	volume	
	weight	

erators, vacuum sweepers, and other machines for the home. The electronics and entertainment departments have televisions, radios, stereos, cameras, recorders, and even computers.

• *Catalogues*. Some department stores have a special catalogue department offering many different products for sale. You can look at the catalogue in the store to find what you want and make your order there. You also can buy a catalogue for a small fee and take it home. Then you can call on the telephone to order what you want. You must wait several days before your order will be ready. Then you pick it up.

• *Specialty shops*. These stores are usually so small that you can find your away around without much trouble. Like other stores, specialty shops try to organize things that are alike in the same area.

TYPES OF STORES

Convenience store. Convenience stores can be found in most neighborhoods. A convenience store sells some groceries, snack food, gasoline, and a few things for the house and car. It is a quick-stop store for when you're in a hurry. You'll probably find that the convenience store's groceries are more expensive than the groceries in a large supermarket. However, the gasoline may be cheaper than at a regular service station.

Grocery store. A grocery store sells groceries. Groceries include food, personal-care products (like shampoo and aspirin), cleaning supplies (like laundry detergent), and paper products (like toilet paper) for your home.

Supermarket. Like a grocery store, a supermarket sells groceries. But it may also sell many other things, like car supplies, furniture, yard-care products, hardware supplies, and toys. Many supermarkets also have a bakery, a small restaurant or delicatessen, and a pharmacy.

Drugstore. Drugstores sell personal-care products and medicines. They also sell cleaning supplies, paper products, yard-care products, and a few kinds of food. Drugstores always have a pharmacy where you can get special medicines.

Department store. Department stores have many different sections (called "departments") that sell things like clothing, furniture, appliances, dishes, and toys.

Discount stores and factory outlets. Discount stores are a mixture of drugstore and department store. They sell many different kinds of products at prices that are lower than department store prices. Factory outlet stores are owned by companies that make products. They sell their own products for less money than you would pay at a regular store.

Specialty shops. There are stores that sell one kind of product—like sports supplies, shoes, cooking supplies, or books. They can be fun to explore. Some specialty shops have catalogues for customers to order from.

Shopping centers and malls. These are large buildings that contain many different kinds of stores—mostly department stores and specialty shops. They also have restaurants, hair salons, game arcades, movie theaters, and doctor's offices.

Understanding how things are measured

• *Packaged products.* Some packaged products are measured as units—like a *loaf* of bread or a *carton* of eggs. Others are measured by volume or by weight. (The system of volume and weight measurements used in the United States is different from the system used in other parts of the world. Appendix B has a chart showing how to match the United States system with others.)

• *Produce.* Most fruits and vegetables are measured by weight.

• *Clothing and shoes.* Clothing and shoes come in many different sizes. Every age group has its own size measurement system. There are sizes for babies, for children, for teenagers, and for adults. There are also sizes for people who are either very small or very large. The size measurement systems are different for boys and girls and for men and women. The size measurement system used in the United States is different from the systems used in other parts of the world.

When you're buying clothing or shoes, you may try items on before you buy them. If you don't know your size, ask a salesclerk to help. If you want shoes, you can try them on while sitting in the shoe department. If you want clothing, you may take several things into a dressing room to try them on privately. Some stores have rules about how many articles of clothing you can take into a dressing room at one time.

Understanding how things are priced

Before buying something, you'll want to know how much it will cost. Here's some information to help you understand how things are priced.

• *Packaged products*. When buying items that are packaged—in boxes, jars, bottles, or cans—you may find the price in two places. First, look on the shelf near the product. The price will be written on a small sign or label. A price sticker is usually placed somewhere on the package also, but not always. Many grocery stores and supermarkets do not mark the price on each package. Instead, the cashier has a computer "scanner" which reads a price code printed on the package. If a product is on sale for a lower price, usually a sign will tell you. For example: "Two for the price of one" or "Save 25 cents."

• *Produce*. Fresh fruits and vegetables are sold in two ways. Sometimes the price is for one item. Other times, the price is by weight. If the price is by weight, you can figure out the total price. Just weigh what you want to buy in a scale and multiply the weight times the price per unit of weight. Grocery stores and supermarkets always have weighing scales in their produce departments.

• *Clothing*. In stores where clothing is sold, every item is marked. Most articles of clothing have a price tag attached. Shoes usually have a price sticker on the bottom. Sometimes, products will be on sale. If they are, a large sign nearby will tell you. The sign may say something like "15% Off," "Reduced 20%," or "Half Price." Sometimes you must figure out what the sale price is. For example, if you want to buy a dress priced at $40 that is "reduced 20%," you will pay $32. Sometimes the price on the tag has been marked out and the new sale price is written there. If you are confused, ask the salesclerk to tell you the price you will pay.

• *A note about sales tax*. Be sure to remember that a sales tax may be added to the price written on the product you want to buy. You will have to pay sales tax on things like clothing, personal-care supplies, and toys. But you won't have to pay tax for most food (except food you buy at a restaurant). The amount of tax will be a percentage of the cost. For example, if you buy a radio for $100, you will pay an extra $10 in tax if the tax rate is 10 percent. Tax rates vary. Ask a salesclerk to tell you what the tax rate is where you live.

Paying for your purchase

When you have chosen what you want to buy, you must pay for it. Different stores take care of this in different ways.

• *Where to pay*. After you have made your choices, take the items you want to buy to a cashier. In grocery stores, supermarkets, drugstores, and discount stores, you'll find rows of cashiers near the front of the store. Sometimes you'll have to wait in line.

In department stores, look for a cashier in each department. For example, if you are in the toy department, you may have to pay for the toys you want before you go on to the housewares department.

Specialty shops are usually so small that they have only one cashier near the front of the store.

• *How to pay*. The cashier will add up the prices for your choices, add the tax, and tell you the total amount you owe. You can pay with cash, a check, or a credit card. If you write a check, you will probably be asked to show your driver's license and a credit card. The clerk will write your driver's license number and your credit card number on the check. If the check bounces, the store will use your driver's license number and your credit card number to find you and make you pay. You will also have to pay the store an extra fee. You usually cannot use a credit card to buy groceries.

Many department stores offer their own credit cards. Ask a cashier where to find an application form.

GOING SHOPPING: A SAMPLE CONVERSATION

Juan and Maria Guerrera are shopping for the family groceries at the Big Town supermarket.

Juan: Didn't you say you wanted to buy some cereal?

Maria: Yes, I want to get some cornflakes.
Juan: Here are cereals, on aisle five. Which brand do you want?
Maria: I want to get the cheapest kind.
Juan: Well, here are two kinds. These two boxes are the same weight, but this one costs five cents less.
Maria: Let's get the bigger box. It is twice the amount but costs less than twice as much, so it is cheaper than the smaller box.
Juan: What else do we need?
Maria: I want some milk and butter. Let's go to the dairy section. It's in the last aisle.

Juan and Maria get the products they need in the refrigerated dairy section. Juan needs one more thing.
Juan: Wait, I need some oil for the car.
Maria: The oil is on aisle nine. What brand do you want?
Juan: Oh, I use any brand, but I need 10-40 weight. I'll get this quart for $1.59. It seems to be the cheapest.
Maria: Is that it?
Juan: Yes, that's all I need. Let's get in line for the cashier.

BUYING CLOTHING: A SAMPLE CONVERSATION

Maria and her daughter Letty are at the shopping mall. They want to buy some school clothes for Letty, who will start high school next week. The first store they go into is a department store.
Letty: Oh, look, Mama. Isn't this a beautiful necklace? It only costs $11. Everybody has them. Can I have one, too?
Maria: We'll see. First, we have to get you a pair of jeans and some shirts to wear to class. Let's see how much they cost.
Letty: But, Mama . . . !
Maria: We have $55 to spend. If we can get you a pair of jeans and two shirts for less than that, we'll buy the necklace.
Letty: Okay.
Maria: Here is the teenage department. I see the jeans on the rack over there.
Letty: Oh, Mama! Janice has a pair just like this. Aren't they wonderful?
Maria: How much do they cost?
Letty: Oh no! They're $69. That's too expensive.
Maria: That's a lot of money for one pair of jeans. Do you want to look at shirts while we're here?
Letty: Yes. Oh, look at this purple one! I love it!
Maria: Well, how much is it?
Letty: It's $36. Mama, we'd better find a different store. I want that necklace more than I want expensive jeans and shirts.
Maria: Okay. Let's go to a different department store. I know one where they have a catalogue department. It seems like the clothes there are less expensive than in this store.

Maria and Letty walk to the other end of the mall and go into a less expensive department store.
Letty: Here's the catalogue department. They sure have pretty things in their catalogues, Mama. Here are the jeans. Look, they have a pair for $14.99. That's better. They look just like the first pair we saw, except they don't have the label on the back. I don't need the label. And look at these shirts! They're having a special. I could buy two shirts for $20. Then I could get the necklace, couldn't I?
Maria: Well, let's see. $14.99 plus $20 is $34.99 or about $35. The necklace is $11, which brings us to $46. The sales tax on everything will be about $3, making a total of $49. Yes. That would work.
Letty: How do we order these clothes?
Maria: Well, we have to take a number and wait until a salesclerk is available. Why don't you get a number for us.
Letty: Here. We're number 83. It looks like they are at number 79 right now. We have to wait, but it shouldn't be long. Oh, Mama, I'm so glad I get the necklace! Can I go get it right now while you order the clothes?
Maria: No, you stay here with me. We have $6 left in our budget. We can get a snack and then buy the necklace on the way to the car. What do you think?
Letty: Okay, that's a good idea. Thanks, Mama. I'm going to love starting high school with my new necklace!

LANGUAGE SKILLS

When you go shopping, you must ***compare*** products. You must know what you want to buy and how much you want to buy. We use naming words to tell *what*. We use naming words and describing words to show *quantity* (how much or how many).

In this chapter you will learn two important language skills for ***comparing*** items:

- How to use naming words to talk about products.
- How to use describing words to talk about different things.

Using Naming Words

In this chapter you will learn two things about naming words.

- Most naming words can either name *one thing* (these are called singular) or they can name *more than one thing* (these are called plural).
- Most naming words that cannot be made plural can still show *how much* in a *specific* or *general* amount.

One and more than one. One way to show how many things you want is to talk about one thing (singular) and more than one thing (plural). To form a plural, add an **s** to the end of the naming word.

Examples:

Singular (one thing)	*Plural (more than one)*
apple	apples
banana	bananas
skirt	skirts
shoe	shoes
store	stores

Showing how much. Many words that name kinds of food, like cheese and bread, are not usually made plural. But we can still say how much of them we want. To do this, we use words that show *quantity*.

Examples: *package* of cheese
loaf of bread
box of cereal

TO LEARN MORE ABOUT NAMING WORDS, STUDY CHAPTER 17.

Exercise 4.1

Here is a conversation between Su and Li Chong. They are shopping at the mall. They talk about many things. Mark the sentence with an "O" if they talk about *one* item. Mark the sentence with an "M" if they talk about *more than one*. The first sentence has been done for you. (The answer key is on page 187.)

Su: (1) I want to buy a **blouse**, Li. O

Li: (2) I need to buy a **suit**. ___

Su: (3) You need the suit for work. You also need a **shirt**. ___

Li: (4) Let's look at **suits** first. I don't know if I have enough money to buy both a suit and a shirt. ___

Su: (5) Do you want a suit or a **jacket**? ___

Li: (6) If I just buy a jacket, I can get two **shirts** too. ___

Su: (7) I'm hungry. Let's forget the clothes and buy **sandwiches**. ___

Li: (8) You'd rather have **cake** than clothes.

Su: (9) You always make me come shopping when I'm hungry. Then I want to eat, not shop. I save a lot of **dollars** that way! ___

Li: (10) Let's go to one more **shop**. Then we can eat. ___

Su: (11) I could have finished shopping and had lunch in a few **minutes** if I had come alone. ___

Li: (12) I've got an **idea**! You eat lunch. I'll buy my suit. ___

Su: (13) What a good idea! Maybe while I'm eating, you could buy me a couple of **blouses**! ___

Li: (14) I get it! You want me to do your shopping, too. Will you try to eat my **lunch** for me? ___

Su: (laughing): (15) Let's go home. I don't want a **meal** or clothes. ___

Using Describing Words

There are other ways of talking about general amounts. We can use special describing words that set limits (limiting words). These words give us a general idea of how much. Use the following list of words:

each	every	all	some	many
much	any	few	more	less

- **Each** and **every** refer to *only one thing*. These words are used with singular naming words.

  Examples: *each dress*
  every shop

- **All, some, many, any,** and **few** refer to *more than one thing*. They are used with plural naming words.

  Examples: *all dresses*
  some shoes
  many coats
  any bananas
  few apples

- **All, some, much, any, more,** and **less** are used with naming words that refer to a quantity of something.

  Examples: *all sugar*
  some milk
  much flour
  any cheese
  more coffee
  less butter

Note: Notice that **all, some,** and **any** can be used with either *quantity* naming words or *plural* naming words.

- We can also use all of these words—except **every**—without a naming word. In that case, we use them *instead of* the naming word.

Examples:

I bought *some cheese.*	I didn't find *any sugar.*
or	or
I bought *some.*	I didn't find *any.*
I didn't use *much flour.*	I don't want *any coffee.*
or	or
I didn't use *much.*	I don't want *any.*

TO LEARN MORE ABOUT DESCRIBING WORDS, STUDY CHAPTER 19.

Exercise 4.2

The sentences below each have a limiting word used with a naming word. Rewrite the sentences using *only* the limiting word. The first sentence has been done for you. (The answer key is on page 187.)

1. Did you buy any blouses, Li?
   I bought **many** blouses. ____I bought many.____
2. Did you use much flour in the cake?
   I used **some** flour. ____________
3. Did you drink more milk than Li did?
   I drank **more** milk. ____________
4. Li chose **many** blouses. ____________
5. Li bought one of **each** kind. ____________
6. Do you have any money?
   I don't have **any** money. ____________
7. Do you need any sugar for the fruit?
   I don't need **much** sugar for the fruit. ____________
8. Is there some butter in the house?
   There isn't **any** butter. ____________
9. Do you need less flour for the bread than for the cake?
   I need **less** flour for the bread. ____________
10. I need **more** eggs for the cake. ____________

Practice

Make up sentences that compare different items. Be sure that you make up sentences that:

- Use singular and plural naming words.
- Use naming words that show quantity.
- Use describing words that limit. Be sure some of the sentences use the describing words *in front of* naming words. Be sure the *other* sentences use describing words *instead of* naming words.

CHAPTER FIVE

Sending Letters and Packages/Requesting

The mail will help you to stay in touch with your friends and families—both here and in your native country. It also will help you to take care of important business—like paying bills and dealing with government offices. Here are some tips to help you:

- Find the post office.
- Learn what the post office can do.
- Mail your letters and packages.

Find the post office

In towns and small cities, there is probably only one post office. But in large cities there will be many post offices. You'll want to find the one nearest you. The quickest way may be to look in the telephone book under "Government Offices." In the alphabetical listing, find "Postal Service." Then call the first number listed and ask the location of the post office that is closest to your home or job.

Learn what the post office can do

The post office is part of the government. Most postal clerks are very helpful, so feel free to ask questions. As you look around the inside of the post office, you'll notice several things:

- Rows of numbered boxes set in the wall. These are post office boxes that people rent. The post office delivers mail to them here. People get their mail by using a key to unlock the box from the front. If you want to rent a post office box, ask a postal clerk.
- Drawers or slots in the wall. You put letters that are ready to mail into these drawers or slots. They usually have signs telling you which kind of mail to put in each one:

USEFUL WORDS

Action words	Naming words	Describing words
to send, to mail	post office	certified
to receive, to get	letter	registered
to register	package	insured
to certify	post office box	stamped
to sign for	mailbox	metered
to deliver	mail delivery	express
to pick up	postal carrier, mail carrier	overnight
to stamp (an envelope)	postal clerk	local
to seal (an envelope)	postage	out-of-town
to insure	Parcel Post	foreign
	return receipt	damaged
	insurance	
	stamps (books, rolls, sheets)	
	postal scale	

Local means mail being sent to someone who lives in your town or city.

Out-of-town means mail being sent to someone who lives outside your town or city.

Metered means mail that has been through a metering machine instead of being stamped. Businesses often use metering machines.

Foreign airmail means mail that is going to another country.

- A machine that sells stamps. Put in the correct amount of money, and the machine will give you stamps.
- A long counter with one or more postal clerks standing behind it. In some post offices, people must wait in line while the postal clerks help other customers. Other post offices use a take-a-number system. When you go in, take a number from a machine and go to the counter when that number is called.
- Tables or counters for customers to use for preparing their mail.
- Boxes of forms you can start filling out as you wait in line, if you already know what forms you need.
- Sometimes, a coin-operated copy machine for your use.

The post office offers many services. To use these services, go to a window and tell a postal clerk what you want to do.

- *Postage to a foreign country.* Letters and packages sent to a foreign country must follow the postal rules of both this country and the country they are being mailed to. Sometimes those rules are unusual. *Before* you prepare your package, ask a postal clerk to tell you the rules that apply. There are rules about what you can send, how large packages can be, and how packages must be prepared.

• *Money orders.* You can use a post office money order to send money to someone. There is a small fee, which varies according to the amount of the money order.

• *Registered mail.* Registered mail is the most secure type of mail. It is expensive because post office employees must give it special attention. Some items must be sent by registered mail, such as cash, irreplaceable items, expensive antiques and jewelry, or stocks and bonds. For an extra fee you can get a return receipt that tells you the person received the package.

• *Certified mail with return receipt requested.* Certified mail with return receipt requested makes sure that *only* the person you sent the mail to can receive it. The person who receives it must sign a form before the mail carrier will give it to him or her.

• *Insurance.* The post office will insure packages sent through the mail. This insurance will pay you for anything that is broken while it is in the mail. If your package arrives with damaged contents, you can collect the insurance money by taking these three things to a postal clerk:

1. A copy or the original of the receipt given when the package was mailed.
2. The damaged item in its package.
3. Something that shows the value of the item.

• *Express Mail.* With Express Mail, packages and letters can be sent between most cities in this country in just one day. Sometimes from smaller towns the mail service takes two days. This service is expensive. International Express Mail will delivery your letters and packages faster than airmail or regular mail, but not the next day. The cost is based on how far away the country is and how much your letter or package weighs.

• *Tracing.* If a letter or package is not received, you can ask the post office to search for it.

• *Postal supplies.* The post office sells basic stamps as well as postcards and envelopes with postage already printed on them. It also sells padded envelopes, boxes, and tubes of different sizes that you can use to pack things in for mailing. It also sells many kinds of stamps to commemorate people and events and special stamps for stamp collectors.

HOW TO MAIL A PACKAGE

• Before you mail a package to a foreign country, ask a postal clerk to tell you the rules that apply for that country.

• You will need to know the size of the package. Measure how *long* the package is. Then measure how *wide* it is (this is called its "girth").

• Pack your box carefully. Use a strong, heavy box. You can buy one at the post office or you can get a used box for free from a grocery or liquor store. Put plenty of crushed newspaper or other stuffing inside, especially around anything that might break. Then tape the box shut. You may also need to wrap the box with brown paper. Cover all seams with tape.

• Use one side of the box for the address. Address the box the same way you address a letter. Be sure to write very clearly in dark ink. If you are sending something that might break, write "FRAGILE" in large letters on the box in several places.

• Take the box to a postal clerk at the post office. Let the postal clerk weigh the box and put the postage on.

Mail your letters and packages

The hours the post office is open are generally posted on the door. Sometimes the post office is closed one afternoon a week. Usually, it's also open late one evening a week and perhaps Saturday mornings to help people who can't come in during working hours.

If you arrive when the post office is busy, you may have to wait. Take your time at the window, even if others are waiting. Ask any questions you may have. Have the clerk tell you the cheapest and the most expensive ways to send your mail. Sometimes the price is not too different, but the time it takes to get there is *very* different. Here are some of the different "classes" of postal service you might use:

- *First Class*. For most letters and packages that you want to arrive quickly. If your letter or package weighs more than a certain amount, it is called Priority Mail. First Class Mail and Priority Mail are basically the same thing.

- *Airmail*. For letters and packages to other countries that you want to arrive more quickly than they would with regular First Class service.

- *Parcel Post*. For all kinds of packages.

- *Book Rate*. For packages that have only books in them.

PICKING UP A PACKAGE: A SAMPLE CONVERSATION

Ming Woo has found a notice from the post office in her mailbox. It says that a package addressed to her is waiting at the post office. Ming takes the notice to the post office. Many people are waiting, so she gets in line to wait also. When it is her turn, Ming walks up to the postal clerk at the counter.

***Clerk*:** May I help you?

Ming: Yes. I should have a package here. Could you get it for me? Here is my notice.

Clerk: Okay. Will you wait just a minute? (He leaves and returns with a box.) Here it is. Would you please sign on this line? (Ming signs.) Anything else?

Ming: Yes. Could you show me some stamp books? I want one for my brother's birthday. He's a stamp collector and is very interested in American stamps.

Clerk: Here are several. Maybe he'd like this one.

Ming: I think you are right. He is very interested in stamps that are about history. Will I have any trouble sending this book to Taiwan?

Clerk: Let me check. (The clerk checks the rules for sending packages to Taiwan.) No, you won't have any trouble.

Ming: How much will it cost for the book and for mailing by International Express Mail?

Clerk: The Commemorative Mint Set is $14.50. The postage will be about $18, or a little more if you sent it Express Mail.

Ming: Thank you. I'll think about that.

Clerk: Thank you. Have a nice day!

SENDING A PACKAGE: A SAMPLE CONVERSATION

Ming returns to the post office in one week. She wants to buy her brother the stamps and send them to him. She also wants to get a money order for a dress she's ordering and mail it with her order form.

Clerk: Hello. How may I help you?

Ming: First, I'd like to buy a 1990 Commemorative Mint Set of stamps. Do you have any left?

Clerk: Yes, we do. Here it is. Will one be enough?

Ming: Yes. But I'd like to send it by International Express Mail so my brother can get it before his birthday. I brought some paper to wrap it. Do you have a special box I can send it in?

Clerk: Yes. Please fill this out. Put your name and address here. Put his name and address over here. Why don't you do everything over at that table and bring it back when you're ready.

Ming takes everything to the table. First, she wraps the stamp collection in birthday wrapping. She tapes a birthday card to the package. Then she puts the birthday package inside the International Express Mail box. She writes her name and address and her brother's name and

address on the mailing form. Then she returns to the window.
Clerk: Okay. I'll just stick the mailing form here on the box and give you a copy as a receipt. Is there anything else?
Ming: Yes. I'd like a money order for $24.
Clerk: Sure. (He does some paperwork.) Here you are. Anything else?
Ming: No. That's everything.
Clerk: Okay. Your total is $56.50.
Ming: Can you change a $100 bill?
Clerk: Sure. Your change is $43.50.
Ming: Thank you.
Clerk: Have a nice afternoon.

LANGUAGE SKILLS

When you go to the post office to mail letters and packages, you must often ***make requests***. You must ask the postal clerk for information or for postal supplies. In this chapter, you will learn three important language skills for ***making requests***:

- How to use helping words with action words to show time or condition.
- How to use naming words to show ownership.
- How to use substitute naming words.

Using Action Words

When you are sending letters and packages, you will need to use some helping words with your action words. These helping words indicate how *definite* the action is. They show *possibility*. In this chapter you will learn to use four helping words:

would can could may

- **Would** can do two things.
  - Tell about something that might happen *under certain conditions*.
    Example: I *would* send them if it wasn't raining.
  - Ask about the *possibility* of something happening.
    Example: *Would* you please sign on the line?

- **Can** can do two things.
  - Tell something that is *able* to happen. (It does not say definitely that the thing *will* happen.)
    Example: I *can* send the package. (I am able to do it.)
  - Ask *if* something is able to happen.
    Example: *Can* you send the package for me tomorrow?

Note: *Can* asks if you are *able* to do something, not if you *will* do it.

- **Could** can do two things.
  - Tell something that might *possibly* happen.
    Example: The package could arrive today. (It is *possible*, not *definite*.)
  - Ask *if* something might possibly happen.
    Example: Could the package arrive today? (It is *possible*?)

- **May** can do two things.
  - Tell something that *might* happen. (The person doing the action has a choice.)
    Example: I *may* send the package.
  - Ask if it is *possible* or *all right* that something might happen.
    Example: *May* I look at the address?

Note: *May* and *could* are very much alike. But *may* suggests that *the person involved* can decide if the action will happen. *Could* suggests that *something else* will decide if the action will happen.

TO LEARN MORE AOUT USING HELPING WORDS WITH ACTION WORDS, STUDY CHAPTER 18

Exercise 5.1

Change the following sentences from statements to questions. The first one has been done for you. (The answer key is on page 187.)

1. You can take this package to the post office tomorrow. ____________________
   Can you take this package to the post office tomorrow?
2. You can send it to my mother. ____________________
   ____
3. I would give you the address if I knew it. ____________________
   ____
4. He could help me if he had time. ____________________
   ____
5. We can find the post office. ____________________
   ____
6. We could find the post office if we had a map. ____________________
   ____
7. I may have the envelope. ____________________
   ____
8. I would mail the letter if I had time. ____________________
   ____
9. She could pick up the mail, if she isn't too busy. ____________________
   ____
10. He may buy insurance for the package. ____________________
    ____

Using Naming Words

Naming words are very flexible. They can be changed to show that something belongs to someone. They can also be replaced by a substitute naming word. The substitute naming words can *also* be changed to show that something belongs to someone.

Using naming words to show belonging or ownership

- To show that something belongs to *one person*, use the naming word followed by **'s**.

Examples:

Naming word (one person)	*Naming word* **+'s**
boy	boy's letter
Amal	Amal's mailbox
mother	mother's address
teacher	teacher's package

• To show that something belongs to *more than one person,* use the naming word for more than one plus the mark **'**.

Examples:

Naming word (more than one person)	*Naming word +'*
boys	boys' letters
mothers	mothers' money orders
doctors	doctors' addresses

Using substitutes for naming words

• Use **he** or **him** to refer to a boy or man.

Example: *Pedro* has the package.
He has the package.
I gave the package to *him*.

• Use **she** or **her** to refer to a girl or woman.

Example: *The woman* bought the stamps.
She bought the stamps.
Pedro asked *her* if he could have one.

• Use **it** to refer to a thing.

Examples: *The box* is ready. *It* is ready.
She has *the box*. She has *it*.

• How do you know when to use **she** or **her, he** or **him**?

- Use **she** or **he** if the person is *doing something.*

Examples:

Naming word	*Substitute naming word*
Maria mailed the letter.	*She* mailed the letter.
The boy has the address.	*He* has the address.

- Use **him** or **her** if something is *being done to the person.*

Examples:

Naming word	*Substitute naming word*
Mary gave *the boy* the letter.	Mary gave *him* the letter.
The mailman brought *Anna* the stamps.	The mailman brought *her* the stamps.
Rosa saw *the mailman.*	Rosa saw *him.*
Mary asked *the postal clerk* about stamps.	Mary asked *him* about stamps.

Using substitute naming words to show ownership

His, **her** or **hers**, and **its** show that something *belongs to* a person or thing. Use **her** *in front of* a naming word to show ownership. Use **hers** *after* a word like *is, was,* or *will be* to show ownership.

Examples:

Naming word	*Substitute naming word*
The letter is *Mary's.*	The letter is *hers.*
Mary's letter is here.	*Her* letter is here.

Naming word	*Substitute naming word*
John's address is new.	*His* address is new.
That is *the man's* package.	That is *his* package.
The letter's address is wrong.	*Its* address is wrong.

TO LEARN MORE ABOUT NAMING WORDS, STUDY CHAPTER 17.

Exercise 5.2

Underline the correct word to show if the person *did something* or if something was *done to* the person. The first one has been done for you. (The answer key is on page 188.)

1. **[He] [Him]** mailed the letter.
2. The package came to **[he] [him]**.
3. **[She] [Her]** bought money orders often.
4. The clerk spoke to **[he] [him]**.
5. **[He] [Him]** answered the clerk.
6. The package was for **[he] [him]**.
7. The package is addressed to **[she] [her]**.
8. **[He] [Him]** talked to the postal carrier.
9. **[She] [Her]** asked the postal carrier about the mail delivery.
10. The postal carrier gave **[she] [her]** the mail.

Exercise 5.3

Choose *his, her, hers,* or *its* to substitute for the highlighted word. The first one has been done for you. (The answer key is one page 188.)

1. **Mary's** package is missing. her
2. The **boy's** letter was returned. _______
3. The **dog's** package had a bone in it. _______
4. The **letter's** seal was broken. _______
5. The **mother's** package arrived late. _______
6. The **package's** address was wrong. _______
7. The **woman's** advice was helpful. _______
8. The **post office's** location is hard to find. _______
9. The **money order's** envelope was open. _______
10. The **lobby's** floor was full of spilled mail. _______

Underline the correct word to show if *one person* or *more than one person* owns something. The first one has been done for you.

11. His **[mother's] [mothers']** letter was returned.
12. Her **[father's] [fathers']** package arrived late.
13. One **[boy's] [boys']** letter came today.
14. One **[letter's] [letters']** address was wrong.
15. One **[clerk's] [clerks']** line was long.

Practice

Make up sentences and questions that make a request of someone. Be sure to use the helping words *would, can, could,* and *may*. In your sentences, use naming words and substitute naming words to show belonging. Also use the substitute naming words *he, she, him, her,* and *it* in place of naming words.

CHAPTER SIX

Eating in a Restaurant/Recommending

Eating out in restaurants makes life easier and more fun. To have a good experience in a restaurant, you must feel at ease. This country has a wide variety of restaurants offering many kinds of food. Here are some tips to help you:

- Pick the type of restaurant you want.
- Dine in different kinds of restaurants.

Pick the type of restaurant you want

What kind of dining experience do you want? Do you want something fast and inexpensive—like a hamburger or a pizza? Do you want a wonderful dinner in a beautiful setting? Here are some of the different kinds of restaurants you have to choose from:

- *Fast-food restaurant or delicatessen*. These serve food that is prepared quickly and easily. Sometimes, the food is already prepared and ready to be served to you. You order, pay for, and pick up your food at a counter. You can get your food to go, or you can sit down in the informal dining room.
- *Cafeteria*. In cafeterias, the food is already prepared and ready to be served. You simply pick what you want to eat and then take it to a table in the dining room. You pay the cashier for your food as you leave the cafeteria.
- *Cafe, diner, or restaurant*. In these dining places, you sit at a counter, at a table, or in a booth. A waiter or waitress comes by to take your food order and serves it to you. He or she also gives you your bill, which you pay to the cashier on your way out of the restaurant.

However, some restaurants are different in a

USEFUL WORDS

Action words	Naming words	Describing words
to sit down, to be seated	restaurant	fast-food
to order (food, a meal)	cafeteria	family-style
to eat, to dine	cafe	dine-in
to tip, to leave a tip	delicatessen	take-out
to reserve, to make	diner	to go
a reservation	reservation	all you can eat
to eat out, to go out to	meal	on the side
eat	breakfast	extra
to be hungry, to have	lunch	expensive
an appetite	dinner	inexpensive, cheap
to recommend, to make	salad bar	spicy
a recommendation	appetizer	bland, mild
	entree	hearty, heavy
	side order	light
	buffet	rich
	sandwich	fried
	dessert	baked
	drink, beverage	broiled
	waiter, waitress	roasted
	bill, check	steamed
	order	grilled
	special	stewed
	menu	hot
	napkin	cold
	silverware, utensils	formal
	glass, cup	informal
	dish, plate	
	kitchen	
	tip, gratuity	
	table	
	booth	

few important ways: Food and drink are more expensive than at other restaurants. You might need to make a reservation to eat there. And you pay your bill to the waiter or waitress, who takes it to the cashier for you and brings back your change.

After you know the kind of restaurant you want to eat at, you must choose a restaurant that is right for you:

- Explore the restaurants near your home. Walk in, look around, and decide if you want to stay. You don't have to eat there just because you walk in. If the restaurant is dirty or not nice for some reason, don't stay. There are plenty of good, clean restaurants.
- Take the advice of a friend who has been to a particular restaurant. Ask your friend all about the restaurant before you go, such as how expensive it is, whether the dress is formal or informal, and where it is located.

• Look in the yellow pages of the telephone book under "Restaurants." You'll find them listed alphabetically, but in larger cities they may also be grouped by the type of food they serve. So if you're looking for Mexican food, you can find all the Mexican restaurants in a single list.

• Read restaurant reviews in the newspaper or in the city or state magazine. Many newspapers and magazines carry restaurant reviews, which are the opinions of a person who has been to the restaurant. Most often, the newspapers and magazines use stars to show the quality of the restaurant. One star is not very good, but four or five stars means the restaurant is one of the best.

Dine in different kinds of restaurants

The rules and practices are different in different kinds of restaurants. If you know what to expect, you will feel more comfortable. Here are some of the things you can expect:

• *Fast-food Restaurants.* In a fast-food restaurant, you walk up to a counter and order your food from a server/cashier. There may be a line—or several lines if there are several cashiers. Just stand at the end of the line and wait until it is your turn to order. The menu is usually hanging on the wall near the counter. You pay for your food when you order it.

The server may give you your food right away, or he may give you an order number. If you get an order number, just step away from the counter and wait for your number to be called. Usually you must go back to the counter to get your food, but some fast-food restaurants bring it to your table. Your food will be on a tray, unless you ordered it to go. If you eat at the restaurant, it is good manners to throw away your trash when you are finished.

Many fast-food restaurants have drive-in windows where you can order your food to go without leaving your car.

• *Restaurants.* When you first walk into some restaurants, you will find a sign that says "Please Wait to Be Seated." Just wait. Someone will come and lead you to a table. In many cities, restaurants offer smoking and nonsmoking sections. The person who seats you may ask if you want smoking or nonsmoking. In other restaurants, you can walk in and sit down at any table or booth you want.

When you are seated, a waiter will come with a menu and ask what you want to drink. Be sure to notice signs around the restaurant advertising the daily specials, which are special low prices that day for certain meals. While the waiter gets your drinks, you can read the menu. If you have not decided what you want to eat when the waiter returns, ask for more time. If you want to know how a certain item is cooked,

HOW TO JUDGE GOOD SERVICE FROM A WAITER

A good waiter:

1. Is friendly, but not *too* friendly.
2. Comes to the table as soon as you are seated.
3. Explains the specials and fills your drink order quickly.
4. Helps you solve any special food needs, such as food with no salt.
5. Keeps your drinking glasses and cups filled.
6. Keeps looking toward your table during the meal, so it's easy for you to indicate you need something.
7. Takes away used dishes as they are emptied.
8. Brings the bill near the end of the meal.
9. Picks up the bill with the money as soon as you lay it down.
10. Politely says "thank you" and asks you to come again.

HOW TO FIGURE A TIP

Most often you will want to tip 15 to 20 percent of the total bill. There's an easy way to figure it.

1. Calculate 10 percent of the bill. You can do this in your head by moving the decimal point one place to the left. For example, if your meal was $12.00, 10 percent would be $1.20. That's the amount you pay for the worst service.

2. Double that amount. Twice $1.20 is $2.40. That's the amount you pay for the best service.

3. For usual service, find some amount between $1.20 and $2.40 that is easy to give. Most people would probably give $2.00 because it's easy. A true 15 percent tip would be $1.80, so at $2.00 you have paid just over 15 percent.

or if you want special combinations not on the menu, ask the waiter.

Usually, everyone at a table is served at the same time. An exception is when one person orders only an entree and another orders a full dinner. The dinner may have two parts: a salad or other appetizer served first and the entree served second. The person who ordered a full dinner would eat his or her salad while the other person waits. Then both people would get their entrees at the same time.

During your meal, your waiter should come by your table once or twice to ask if you need anything. If you need help during the meal and the waiter is not there, try to catch his eye by raising one hand slightly. The waiter should immediately come to your table.

After you finish eating, the waiter should clear away the dirty dishes and ask if you want dessert. If you don't want dessert, then he should put your bill on the table. If you do want dessert, then he should put your bill on the table after he clears away your dessert dishes. You may stay and talk as long as you want, even after the waiter has left your bill on the table. However, if the restaurant is very busy and people are waiting for a table, it is polite to leave when you are finished eating.

A waiter's job is to serve you. You will pay for that service. When the meal is finished, you are expected to pay a tip for service. Standard tips are 15 to 20 percent of the total bill before tax. If the service is very bad, you may choose not to leave a tip or to leave only 10 percent. If the service is fine, leave about 15 percent. A 20 percent tip tells the waiter he did an excellent job. Tips do not need to be exact amounts. Leaving pennies in the tip is an insult to the waiter.

If you pay your bill with a credit card, you may add the waiter's tip to the bill. If you pay with cash, put the tip on the table as you leave. The waiter will pick it up.

• *Cafeterias*. In a cafeteria, you will usually find a line of people waiting to choose their food. If so, then get in line behind them. You'll pick up a tray and silverware wrapped in a napkin before you come to the food.

As you walk through the food line, tell the food servers what you want. They will put your choice on a dish and hand you the dish to put on your tray. The prices for all the food items are usually listed on a sign behind the food servers.

At the end of the line, a checkout clerk will give you a bill that adds up your food cost. Most often, you then take your tray to a table and sit down to eat. Afterwards, you leave your dirty dishes on the table and take the bill to a cashier. You must pay your ticket to get out of the restaurant. You do not pay tips in a cafeteria. Most of them don't take checks or credit cards.

• *Fancy Restaurants*. Food and drink at fancy restaurants are usually expensive. They offer the best in food and service. The decor is appealing. People dress up and make the meal a special event.

For fancy restaurants, you must make a reservation. That means you must call ahead to say:

1. What day or evening you are coming.
2. How many people are coming.
3. What time you are coming.

The restaurant will save a table just for you.

DESSERT AND COFFEE AFTER THE MOVIE: A SAMPLE CONVERSATION

Ricardo Rodriguez and Fermina Díaz have just left a movie. They are engaged to be married, but Fermina is still living in another town. She is visiting Ricardo. They have decided to go to a restaurant for dessert and coffee, but they have not decided where to go.

Ricardo: We can go to either a French restaurant or a little cafe I know near my house. At the French restaurant we could have both a chocolate torte and chocolate coffee. I know how much you like the taste of chocolate. At the cafe near my house they don't have chocolate coffee, but they serve a great chocolate pie. What sounds good?

Fermina: Oh . . . . It all sounds so good. I want both the chocolate torte *and* the chocolate pie. (They both laugh.)

Ricardo: Well, if it's too much, we'll go to neither the French restaurant nor the cafe. Why don't we go get ice cream? We could visit our favorite shop, the one on the square.

Fermina: Oh yes. Ice cream would taste so good. But I want it by my chocolate torte and my chocolate pie! (More laughing.)

Ricardo: Well, I think we should go to the French restaurant. You haven't been there before, and you'd like the romantic decor. It smells good and it's beautiful, like you.

Fermina: Okay. Okay. I'm convinced. Let's go!

FRIENDS FOR DINNER: A SAMPLE CONVERSATION

The next night, Ricardo arranged dinner at a fancy Chinese restaurant so his friends Steven James and Susan Henderson could meet Fermina. Ricardo made reservations for 7 P.M. and the four friends met in the lobby of the restaurant. He introduced everyone and they were immediately seated at a table. The waiter brought water to everyone and took their drink orders.

Ricardo: The newspaper rates this the best Chinese restaurant in town. They gave it four stars last week. The restaurant reviewer says the food here is more authentic than at the other Chinese restaurants in town.

Susan: Yes. I read that review. The roasted duck is supposed to be especially good.

Steven: Well, duck isn't my favorite food. I'm definitely sticking with chicken.

Susan: But look at the list of shrimp dishes! You like shrimp.

Fermina: I like shrimp, too. I can't decide between the duck and the shrimp.

Ricardo: In Chinese restaurants, they have a wonderful custom. Each order comes on a big serving dish. We can each order something we want and then share it with everyone. Susan can get the duck, and maybe Fermina and Steven can get two different shrimp dishes. I'll choose a beef dish. Then we can all share.

Steven: Well, if we're going to do that, why don't I get a chicken dish and then we'll have beef, chicken, shrimp, and duck to sample.

Fermina: Oh, I'd like that. Then I can taste everything.

Ricardo: I am so happy to have you all together. I want all the people I care about to know each other. After the wedding, we'll do this often.

Susan: Have you set the wedding date yet?

Fermina: Yes. It'll be two months from yesterday. I have to finish the contract my company has before I can move here. We're going to be married at my mother's house in the . . . Oh, look!

Steven: That is beautiful! Look at those flowers. Are they real? That looks like a real rose on the side.

Susan: No. Those are vegetables. They cut them to look like that. Aren't they wonderful? We can take them home.

Fermina: Our family loves to cook and my mother likes food to be pretty. She'd love the rose.

Ricardo: Maybe we can put it in a plastic bag and you can take it to her.

Fermina: That would be great. Steven, you shared your chicken with us, but you haven't tried the duck. Don't you like the taste?

Steven: No. Don't laugh, but I don't like the smell. (Everyone laughs, anyway.)

Ricardo: How can you not like the smell?

Steven: I think it has to do with my mother cooking a duck in the kitchen when I was a kid. I always remember it when I see duck. I always remember the smell. I hated it.

Fermina: How long since you've actually tasted duck?
Steven: I never did. I didn't when I was a kid and I never have since then.
Susan: Don't you think it's time we ordered some more plum wine? They have the best in town here.
Steven: Maybe if I drank another glass of plum wine, I'd be ready to taste the duck.
Ricardo: That's a deal. (He raises his hand to get the waiter's attention.) We'd like another bottle of plum wine.
Waiter: Of course.
Susan: Fermina, are you and Ricardo going to live in Ricardo's apartment after you're married?
Fermina: No. It's too small. Ricardo is looking for a two-bedroom so we'll have room for guests. Do you have any suggestions?
Susan: Well, the apartment complex I live in is really nice. I think they have some apartments available now. I'll ask tomorrow.
Steven: Hey! This duck is really good. I like it. (Everyone laughs.)
Fermina: Just look what you've been missing out on all these years.
Steven: Well, no more. Duck is great.

The group finishes the meal, pays, and leaves the restaurant. They say good-bye outside.

LANGUAGE SKILLS

When we eat in a restaurant, we often give and get ***recommendations***. We want to know other people's opinions about where and what we should eat—and we give our own opinions to other people about the same things. In this chapter, you will learn two important language skills for making recommendations.

- How to use substitute naming words to talk about more than one person.
- How to use describing words to tell how something *is, looks, smells, sounds,* and *tastes*.

Using Naming Words

In this chapter, you will learn about substitute naming words that talk about more than one person. These substitute naming words are:

we	us	our	ours
they	them	their	theirs

Examples:

Naming word	*Substitute naming word*
Juan and I eat out.	*We* eat out.
Friends join *Juan and me*.	Friends join *us*.
It is *Juan's and my* choice.	It is *our* choice.
The choice is *Juan's and mine*.	The choice is *ours*.
Juan and Rosa like cake.	*They* like cake.
The waiter sees *Juan and Rosa*.	The waiter sees *them*.
Juan and Rosa's table is ready.	*Their* table is ready.
The coats are *Juan's and Rosa's*.	The coats are *theirs*.

- Use **we** and **us** to talk about yourself with others.
  Examples: *We* eat out often.
  The people in the restaurant know *us*.
  - Use **we** if you and the others with you are doing the action.
    Example: *We* are eating lunch.
  - Use **us** if something is being done *to* you and others with you.
    Example: The waiter is bringing *us* the food.

- Use **our** and **ours** to talk about something that belongs to you with others.
  Examples: This restaurant is *our* favorite.
  This lunch is *ours*.
  - Use **our** with a naming word.
    Example: *Our* dessert is on the table.
  - Use **ours** without a naming word after the words *is, are, was,* and *will be*.
    Example: The dessert is *ours*.

- Use **they** and **them** to refer to more than one person, not including yourself.
  Examples: *They* like the restaurant.
  The waiter serves *them*.
  - Use **they** if the people are doing something.
    Example: *They* are ordering dinner.
  - Use **them** if something is being done *to* the people.
    Example: The waiter brought *them* the food.

- Use **their** and **theirs** to talk about something that belongs to more than one person, not including yourself.
  Examples: The restaurant is *their* second home.
  That order is *theirs*.
  - Use **their** with a naming word.
    Example: *Their* dessert is cheap.
  - Use **theirs** without a naming word after the words *is, are, was,* and *will be*.
    Example: That table is *theirs*.

TO LEARN MORE ABOUT SUBSTITUTE NAMING WORDS, STUDY CHAPTER 17.

Exercise 6.1

Underline the correct substitute naming word in each sentence. The first one has been done for you. (The answer key is on page188.)

1. **[<u>We</u>] [Us]** ordered lunch in the restaurant.
2. The waiter gave the menu to **[we] [us]**.
3. **[They] [Them]** drank coffee.
4. The waiter explained the menu to **[we and they] [us and them]**.
5. The waiter has seated **[we] [us]** many times.
6. **[We] [Us]** asked for a breakfast menu.
7. The waiter gave the menu to **[they] [them]** by mistake.
8. **[They] [Them]** found the appetizer too hot.
9. **[We and they] [Them and us]** chose the restaurant together.
10. **[We] [Us]** want to drink only water.

Exercise 6.2

In these sentences, underline the word that shows ownership. The first one has been done for you. (The answer key is on page 188.)

1. The appetizer and dessert are **[<u>ours</u>] [our]**.
2. The salad bar is **[their] [theirs]** favorite.
3. The iced tea is **[our] [ours]** choice.
4. This menu has **[our] [ours]** favorite desserts on it.
5. **[Their] [Theirs]** sandwiches are small.
6. Those sandwiches are **[our] [ours]**.
7. We sit at **[our] [ours]** table every day.
8. They read **[their] [theirs]** menu carefully.
9. That menu is **[their] [theirs]**.
10. This menu is **[our] [ours]**.

Using Describing Words

- Describing words are usually put in one of two places.
  - Before a naming word.
    Example: *Cold* food upsets me.
  - After certain action words.
    Example: The food is *cold*.

- Describing words may come after *these* action words:
  am, is, are, was, were, will be
  smell(s), taste(s), sound(s), feel(s), seem(s)

Examples:
I *am happy* with this restaurant.
That restaurant *is dirty*.
The lunches *are large*.
The food *was hot*.
The lunches *were not cold*.
The room *will be quiet soon*.
The hamburger *smells good*.
The ice cream *tastes cold*.
The music *sounds too loud*.
Sitting down in the restaurant *feels wonderful*.
The side orders *seem expensive*.

TO LEARN MORE ABOUT DESCRIBING WORDS, STUDY CHAPTER 19.

Exercise 6.3

Add one of these words—*am, is, are, was, were, will be, smells, tastes, sounds, feels, seems*—to the words given to make a sentence. The first answer has been done for you. There is more than one word that will work in each sentence. (The answer key is on page 188.)

1. I ____feel____am____was____will be____ hungry.
2. The restaurant ________________ cold.
3. The food ________________ good.
4. This chair ________________ comfortable.
5. The appetizer ________________ small.
6. The food here ________________ cheap.
7. The dessert ________________ extra.
8. The drinks ________________ free.
9. The food ________________ not expensive here.
10. That restaurant ________________ formal.

Practice

Make up sentences that are recommendations. Be sure to make up sentences using *we, us, our, ours, they, them, their,* and *theirs*. Try to make your sentences descriptive by using describing words after these action words: *am, is, are, was, were, will be, smell(s), taste(s), sound(s), feel(s),* and *seem(s)*.

CHAPTER SEVEN

Talking on the Telephone/Apologizing

The telephone is an important tool in our lives. With a telephone, we can find out information, make appointments, and talk with our friends and families. Telephones are everywhere. Most homes and businesses have several. Pay telephones are located inside and outside gas stations and some stores. Here are steps to help you learn to:

- Make a local telephone call.
- Make a long-distance telephone call.
- Use special telephone services.

Make a local telephone call

Telephones come in several types and styles:

- *Rotary-dial telephone*. A telephone with numbers and letters in a circle around a dial. This is an old style telephone.
- *Push-button telephone*. A telephone with a pad of buttons with letters and numbers on them. These are common.
- *Pay telephone*. A telephone that requires you to deposit money before you can make a call. Most pay telephones are push-button phones.

You must take three steps to make a local telephone call:

1. ***Find the telephone number you want.*** You can find the telephone numbers you need in many ways:

- *Use the telephone book.*

White pages. Look up the last name of the person you want to call. People's last names are listed in alphabetical order. Under each last name you will find.

- First name.
- Address.
- Telephone number.

Businesses are listed in the white pages alphabetically under the name of the business.

Yellow pages. Look in the yellow pages for names of businesses and advertisements for businesses. The businesses are not listed alphabetically by name. They are listed under headings that tell:

- The products they sell.
- The services they offer.

For example, you would not look up the telephone number for "Hadda Cab Company" under "H" for "Hadda." It would be listed under "Taxicabs," along with the names, addresses, and telephone numbers of all the other taxicab companies in your area.

- *Emergency telephone numbers.* The first page in the telephone book usually lists emergency telephone numbers. Use them if you need help. Other front pages of the telephone book have information about the telephone company and the services it offers.
- *Dial directory assistance* (or information) and ask the operator for the number you want. Instructions for dialing directory assistance can be found in your telephone book. You must pay a small fee for using directory assistance.
- *Ask friends to give you their telephone numbers.* Write down the numbers and keep them together in a list.

2. ***Make sure you are calling a local telephone number.*** Local telephone numbers will have seven numbers. Look at the first three numbers, which are called the *prefix.* You are making a *local* call if:

- The prefix is the same as the prefix for your telephone number.
- The prefix is listed on the map of local prefixes in the front of your telephone book.

If you accidentally call a prefix that is not in your local calling area, you will get a recording that says, "Your call cannot be completed as dialed." You are not charged for the mistake. If you want to check whether a number is a local call, you can dial "0" and ask the operator. You may be charged a small fee for the service.

3. ***Dial the number.*** Usually, someone will answer the telephone on the other end. However, you may get an answering machine. An answering machine tells you that the person you are calling is not there and asks you to leave a message.

Make a long-distance telephone call

You can make two kinds of long-distance calls: within this country and international.

- ***Within this country*** long-distance calls are those made to places outside your area code. You must arrange for long-distance service with the telephone company when you have your telephone service set up.

You can call long distance two ways:

1. ***Dial directly.*** You can dial the number yourself if you know the area code of the place you are calling. If you don't know it, dial "0" and ask the operator. You will pay a small fee for this service.

2. ***Dial "0" to get the operator*** and ask for assistance in placing the call. You will pay a fee for the help. By using the operator, you can call *station-to-station, person-to-person,* and *collect.*

Station-to-station calls. The operator dials the number for you and connects you. You must pay for the operator's help.

Person-to-person calls. The operator dials the number for you. When someone answers, the operator asks for the person you wish to speak to. You do not pay for the call if you cannot reach the person you want. But you must pay for the operator's help.

Collect calls. The operator dials the number for you. When someone answers, the operator tells your name to the person who answers and asks if he or she will pay for the call. The person can say yes or no. He or she will pay extra for the operator's help.

- ***International calls*** outside this country can be made three ways:

1. Arrange for international calling with your long-distance company. Use the steps they give you.
2. Ask the operator to help you. Dial directory assistance and ask for the code numbers for the country and city you want to call.
3. Dial directly.

USEFUL WORDS

Action words	Naming words	Describing words
to call, to make a call	telephone, telephone set	loud
to be called, to get or have a call	telephone book	soft
to dial (the phone)	telephone number	noisy
to hang up (the phone)	operator	quiet
to connect (phone service)	operator-assisted call	busy
to disconnect (phone service)	toll call	buzzing
to ring	area code	
to be cut off	long-distance	
	telephone line	
	rotary-dial telephone, dial telephone	
	touch-tone telephone, push-button telephone	
	ring	
	directory assistance, information	
	emergency (number, call)	
	hot line	
	toll-free number, 800 number	
	party line	
	pay telephone	
	long-distance calling card	
	telephone bill	
	directory listing	
	white pages, yellow pages, blue pages, green pages (index)	
	nonlisted number, nonpublished number	
	automatic dialing	
	call waiting	
	call forwarding	
	direct-dial call	
	collect calls	
	dial tone	
	prefix	

Use special telephone services

Telephone companies offer many different options you may want to try. You will pay extra fees for these options.

- *Call waiting.* When you are talking on the phone, you can answer another call without hanging up on the first call. You can have two phone calls at the same time.
- *Call forwarding.* When you are away from home, you can change your telephone to make your calls go to the number you are at. When you come home, you can change it back again.
- *Speed calling.* Allows you to make calls to certain phone numbers by dailing only two numbers.

ANSWERING MACHINES

An answering machine takes messages for people when they are away from their telephone or choose not to answer the telephone. If you dial a telephone number and get an answering machine, here's what to do:

1. Listen to the message. Follow the instructions in the message. Most often, messages say to wait for the beep before you start talking. But some machines don't have a beep, so you just begin talking when the message is done.

2. Talk to the machine. It may seem strange at first, but the person you called wants to know that you called. Be sure to tell:

- Your name.
- Your telephone number.
- When you called.
- When to call you back.
- Any information you want the person to know.

3. Hang up.

Perhaps you'd like to have an answering machine at your house. Shop for one at department stores or discount stores. The answering machine will come with instructions about how it works.

CALLING A WRONG NUMBER: A SAMPLE CONVERSATION

José Mirjyn is calling his friend Socorro Barros. He hasn't talked to Socorro in a long time. He dials the number she gave him last summer.

Voice on the line: Hello.

José: Hi, Socorro! It's José Mirjyn.

Voice: Who?

José: José Mirjyn. Uh . . . is this Socorro Barros?

Voice: I'm sorry. There's no one by that name here.

José: Is this 555-1088?

Voice: Yes. But there's no Socorro Barros here.

José: Well, I'm sorry to bother you. I'm trying to reach a friend. Could you tell me how long you've had this number?

Voice: I've had the same number for three years.

José: Well, Socorro gave me this number last summer.

Voice: Oh, then you want to talk to my sister. I was gone last summer. My sister lived here while I was away. Maybe she can help you. (A pause.)

Second voice: This is Lisa Pope. Can I help you?

José: I apologize for being so much trouble, but I'm trying to reach someone I met last summer. Her name is Socorro Barros and she gave me this telephone number last summer. Do you know where I could reach her?

Lisa: Yes, I do. But who are you?

José: I'm sorry. I should have introduced myself before. I'm José Mirjyn. I met Socorro at my sister Estela's house. Do you know Estela Mirjyn?

Lisa: Oh yes. I'm so sorry! I should have recognized your name. Estela works in my office. Socorro and I were at Estela's house last summer helping her get ready for the office party. I remember that you came by before the party to deliver tables. Afterwards, you took them back for us.

José: That's right. I remember meeting you.

Lisa: Well, Socorro stayed with me last summer when I was house-sitting for my sister. Then she moved to her own apartment. Her number is 555-9299. I know she'd be glad to hear from you.

José: Well, thank you for the information. I'm sorry to bother you.

Lisa: No trouble at all. Tell Socorro hello from me.

José: I will. Thank you.

APOLOGIZING: A SAMPLE CONVERSATION

José dials Socorro's telephone number. She answers the telephone.

Socorro: Hello.

José: Hello. Is this Socorro Barros?

Socorro: Yes. Who is this?

José: This is José Mirjyn. I met you last summer at a party at my sister's house.

Socorro: Yes. (Silence on the line.)

José: Socorro, I am calling to apologize. First, I'm sorry I waited so long to call. I should have called you the next day! But I was so embarrassed, I just couldn't then. It's been almost six months since the party and I am still thinking about you. I am still so ashamed of myself. So I finally decided to call you to let you know how I feel.

Socorro: Well, I am glad you did. We had so much fun during the party. Then afterwards you ruined it all with your insults.

José: Well, that's really why I called. I *am* sorry about what I said. It was rude. I never really meant to be, but I know I was. I want you to know I'm sorry.

Socorro: Well, it really hurt my feelings. I couldn't believe you could suddenly say such a thing! I've been really mad at you ever since. I didn't think I ever wanted to hear from you again.

José: I can't blame you. But I do hope you will accept my apology. I promise it won't happen again.

Socorro: I accept your apology. Can we just forget it now?

José: We can if you'll let me take you to dinner Friday night. Would you like to try the new Italian restaurant on Main Street?

Socorro: I'm sorry, but I can't. I will be helping my brother move that night. I expect we will be carrying boxes until very late.

José: Well, then how about if I help with the moving? I could come after work and bring some hamburgers or pizza for all of us. Then I will help with the moving.

Socorro: That's a wonderful idea. We will finish much quicker with three people working.

José: Good. I will call on Thursday to get directions to your brother's house.

Socorro: Okay. Thank you for calling.

José: Goodbye.

Socorro: Goodbye.

LANGUAGE SKILLS

When you ***apologize,*** you want to put the past away. You want someone to know how you feel *now* and how you will feel *in the future*. In this chapter you will learn three skills you can use when you feel you must ***apologize:***

- How to use action words to tell what you feel now.
- How to use action words to tell about the future.
- How to use connecting words to talk about time.

Using Action Words

• One way to talk about things happening in the present is to use **am, is,** or **are** with an action word that ends in **-ing**.

Examples: I *am feeling* sorry.
She *is hoping* you still care.
We *are wishing* you'd forgive us.

Sometimes we shorten *am, is,* and *are* and connect them with the person doing the action.

- Drop the first letter: *(a)m, (i)s, (a)re.*
- Put in ' instead.
- Add the ' and letter(s) to the naming word.

Examples: *I am* hoping.
I (a)m hoping. (Drop the first letter.)
I 'm hoping. (Put ' for the dropped letter.)
I'm hoping. (Add the ' and letter to the naming word.)

Here are the naming and action words before and after the change:

I am . . . I'm	We are . . . We're
You are . . . You're	It is . . . It's
She is . . . She's	He is . . . He's
José is . . . José's	They are . . . They're
Socorro is . . . Socorro's	The group is . . . The group's

- There are two ways to talk about things that are going to happen.
  - You may use the word **will** + an action word.

    Example: He *will help*.
  - You may use the words **will** + **be** + an action word + **-ing**.

    Example: He *will be helping*.

Note: Sometimes we shorten the word *will* to *'ll*. We add these letters to the word that comes before it.

Examples: He *will help* *He'll help*.
I *will call*. *I'll call*.

TO LEARN MORE ABOUT ACTION WORDS, STUDY CHAPTER 18.

Exercise 7.1

Here are some sentences about things that happened in the past. Change them to take place in the present (now). Write them once using *am, is,* or *are* and a verb that ends in *-ing*. Write them a second time using the short form of the verb. The first one has been done for you. (The answer key is on page 188.)

1. He was feeling bad. ___He is feeling bad. He's feeling bad.___
2. I was wishing we could talk. ______
3. You were thinking of her. ______
4. We were hoping he'd return. ______
5. José was talking to her. ______

Exercise 7.2

Here are some sentences where the action takes place in the present (now). Change the sentence so the action takes place in the future. The first sentence has been done for you. (The answer key is on page 188.)

1. I hope he comes. ___I hope he will come.___
2. She is carrying big boxes. ______
3. Socorro is waiting for his call. ______
4. José is wishing he'd called. ______

5. Estela wants the tables. ______________________________

6. Lisa and Estela work together. ______________________________

7. Socorro and José like each other. ______________________________

8. José calls Socorro. ______________________________

Using Connecting Words

Some connecting words help you talk about time. The following words help you tell *when* something has happened.

now	then	soon	still
first	last	always	never
after	before	during	until
since	often	rarely	finally
also	already	yet	hardly ever
afterwards			

Sometimes these words come at the *beginning* of a sentence.

Examples: *Now,* José wants to apologize.
Then, he was embarrassed.
Finally, he called.

Sometimes these words come in the *middle* of a sentence.

Examples: José wanted to call *after* the party.
José and Socorro had fun *during* the party.
Socorro *always* remembered José.

TO LEARN MORE ABOUT CONNECTING WORDS, STUDY CHAPTER 20.

Exercise 7.3

From the list above, choose two different connecting words to finish the following sentences. (There are many correct answers for each.) Notice how different words change what is said about time. The first one has been done for you. (The answer key is on page188.)

1. Socorro finally forgave José.
   Socorro already forgave José.
2. José __________ remembered Socorro.
   José __________ remembered Socorro.
3. Estela __________ thought the party was fun.
   Estela __________ thought the party was fun.
4. Lisa __________ knew who José was.
   Lisa __________ knew who José was.
5. __________ the party, José took care of tables.
   __________ the party, José took care of tables.
6. __________ José and Socorro can talk.
   __________ José and Socorro can talk.
7. __________ José had to apologize.
   __________ José had to apologize.

Practice

Prepare an apology for someone. Talk about what happened in the past, how you feel now, and what you want the future to be like. Use connecting words that show time to help you explain changes.

CHAPTER EIGHT

Getting Around Town/Suggesting

Whether you are a newcomer to your city or you have lived there for a while, you may not have gotten acquainted with it yet. Your town or city has many things to offer you—interesting places to visit, offices and shops to do business with. To begin to feel at home where you live:

- Learn about your town or city.
- Find ways to travel around town.
- Plan a day around town.

Learn about your town or city

Exploring the place where you live can be an adventure. Even if you've lived in one place for a while, there are probably many things you haven't found. Look for information in the following places:

- *The public library*. Look in the lobby of the library for leaflets about events and places to visit in your city. Ask the librarian:
  - What events the city is known for.
  - What institutions and buildings you might visit.
  - Where to find more information about the city.
- *The chamber of commerce*. Visit the chamber of commerce and pick up its free leaflets. The people there can also answer your questions about the city. To find it, look for the telephone number in the yellow pages of the telephone book under "Chambers of Commerce." Call and ask where it is located.
- *Newspapers and local magazines*. Buy

USEFUL WORDS

Action words	**Naming words**	**Describing words**
to drive	map	north
to ride in (a taxi, car, truck, bus)	road	south
to hire, to rent (a taxicab)	car, automobile	east
to catch (a bus)	bus	west
to read (a map)	highway, freeway	far, distant
to orient, to get oriented	subway	near, close
to be lost, to get lost	taxi, taxicab, cab	tall, high
to locate, to be located	city	short, low
to tour	town	wide, broad
to take an outing, to go on an outing	public library	thin, narrow
to direct, to give directions	landmark	busy, crowded
	chamber of commerce	quiet, empty
	newspaper	fast, speeding
	local magazine	slow, crawling
	parks and recreation department	
	map legend	
	parks	
	museums	
	bus station	
	airport	
	taxi stand	
	bus stop	
	subway station	
	distance	
	mileage	
	route	
	traffic	
	traffic jam	

newspapers and local magazines for their information about the city.

• *Newspapers.* You can find newspapers in newspaper racks outside grocery stores. You can also buy them at large bookstores. On Sundays the newspaper has the most information. Read the stories about and listings of places to go and things to do.

• *Local magazines.* Most cities have their own magazine. If you visit the chamber of commerce, you may get one free. You can often find the local magazine for sale on magazine racks at grocery stores, bookstores, or newsstands. You can also subscribe to the magazine so it will be mailed to you.

• *The parks and recreation department.* Many cities have departments that take care of their parks and other types of recreation, including museums and events. To find information about what your city offers:

HOW TO ORIENT YOURSELF WITH A CITY MAP

A map of your city can tell you many important and helpful things.

- It can show you the major highways that cross the city.
- It can help you locate the downtown area of the city, which is its center. Most cities are built around a courthouse or perhaps a capitol building. Large cities like New York City have several centers.
- Some maps have special signs for recreation areas, such as playgrounds, swimming pools, baseball fields, tennis courts, and recreation centers.
- It can help you find the water in your city. Most maps color rivers and lakes blue. Find any bodies of water in your city. Here, you'll usually find water activities such as boating and water skiing.
- It can show you the major parks in your city. They are usually colored green on maps.

Learn to find streets by finding your home.

- Turn the map over or look at the bottom for a list of street names in tiny print. Notice that the street names are followed by a letter and a number.
- Look up your street name and find the number and letter that follow it.
- Turn back to the map and find the same letter at the top or bottom of the map. Put a ruler straight down (or up) from the letter.
- Find the number on one side of the map. Put another ruler straight right (or straight left) from the number. Where the two rulers meet, look for the name of your street. You should be able to locate where your home is. Mark it on the map.

Continue to explore the map, noticing what each color or symbol is used to show. You should be able to find schools, school districts, counties, and airports on your map.

Call the city. Look in the telephone book for "Government Offices—City." Look for the telephone numbers two ways:

- Find the listing for the "Parks and Recreation" department.

- If there is no listing for "Parks and Recreation," call the main city telephone number. Ask what department or departments your city has for parks, recreation, museums, and activities.

Call these departments. Ask if they offer free leaflets about city activities. Perhaps they will send them to you in the mail, but you may be asked to pick them up yourself.

- *A city map.* Get a city map and orient yourself. Look for a city map in these places:
- At the chamber of commerce, probably free.
- In grocery stores, bookstores, and gas stations, for a small price.

Find ways to travel around town

You can travel around your city in several ways:

- *On foot.* Start with a walking tour of your neighborhood. Be creative. Walk down one side of the street and back on the other side. Visit shops and restaurants and parks along the way, or walk the streets in a circle around your home, always exploring.

Make walking a part of every outing you take. Wear comfortable shoes to explore your city's nature trails, jogging paths, parks, museums, and malls.

- *In a car.* Use your own car to drive around the city. Sometimes it's fun to just drive around without knowing where you're going. Use a city map. In large cities, try not to drive during rush-hour traffic (7–9 A.M. and 4–6 P.M.) until you learn something about the highways.
- *In a city bus.* To make best use of city buses, get a bus schedule with a map of bus

routes. They are usually available at the public library and at other locations around the city. City buses usually cost very little to ride.

• *In a taxicab.* While taxicabs can be expensive, they are occasionally necessary in some cities. There are two ways to get a taxicab:

• In a large city, stand on the curb of the street, watching for a taxicab to pass you. You can recognize a taxicab by the sign across the top of the car. As the taxicab approaches, raise one hand high and wave. Some people whistle and call out, "Taxi!" Sometimes the cab will not stop. Just wait for the next one and do the same thing.

• When you know you want a taxicab at a certain time, you can call on the telephone to order one to pick you up. For example, many people use a taxicab to get to the airport. Look in the yellow pages of the telephone book under "Taxicabs" to find a list of taxicab companies in your town. Call and ask that a taxicab be in front of your house at a certain time. When it's time for the taxicab to arrive, watch for it. Drivers usually will honk their horn, but will not come to your door to tell you they have arrived. You are expected to be waiting and ready to come out.

Charges for taxicab service are based on the distance you travel. A machine called a "meter" in the taxicab keeps track of how far you have gone and what your total cost is. In some places, the area is divided into zones and the price will depend on how many zones you must cross. In addition to the cost, you are expected to pay a tip of 10 to 20 percent. Pay larger tips if the taxicab driver has helped you in any way.

Plan a day around town

Here are some ideas to help you enjoy exploring your city:

• Set aside time to explore the city. If you can't take an entire day, take half a day or a few hours.

• Start with activities you're most interested in. If you're a sports fan, explore the sports facilities first. If you prefer art, visit the art galleries and museums in town.

• Take family and friends with you to explore.

• Don't try to do too many things in one day. It's easier to enjoy outings if you don't have to hurry.

VISITING THE CHAMBER OF COMMERCE: A SAMPLE CONVERSATION

Nazar and Magda Zamora are visiting the chamber of commerce for their city. They enter the office and a woman walks up to them.

Woman: Hello. Can I help you?

Nazar: Yes, thank you. We're looking for information about the city.

Woman: Well, you've come to the right place. Are you interested in anything special?

Magda: We could use a map. Do you have a good map of the city?

Woman: Yes, we do. It's right here and it's free.

Magda: Thank you.

Woman: Are you new in town?

Nazar: We've been here about a month now.

Woman: How do you like it so far?

Magda: Oh, it's a wonderful city!

Nazar: Are there lots of places to swim?

Woman: Oh yes. We have twenty-four pools all over the city. Here is a leaflet from the parks department. It tells you where to find the public pools. This one might help you, too. It tells about the public swimming areas around the lake. People love our beautiful lake.

Nazar: Thank you. This is a great help.

Woman: Please look around and take any of the leaflets you see here. You'll especially want a copy of our city magazine and the newspaper.

Nazar: Thank you for your help.

Woman: You're welcome. I'll be at the desk. Let me know if you need anything else.

PLANNING A TRIP TO THE LAKE: A SAMPLE CONVERSATION

Nazar and Magda want to invite their new friends Anna and James Turner to join them for a day at the lake. They are at home looking at

their map and planning the outing.
Nazar: They live so far away. Do you remember where their house is?
Magda: Isn't it on the north side of town behind that big shopping center? That *is* a long way. We'd have to drive up Highway 14 and then all the way back out Highway 36 to the lake.
Nazar: What if we met them somewhere?
Magda: I think we should have them drive to the Falnel shopping center.
Nazar: They could park their car in the parking lot and wait outside of the center. There is a green awning. They could stand under it to get out of the heat. We could pick them up there. That might work. If we pick them up at the shopping center, we can drive west on Highway 89 until we get to Highway 36. We should be able to make the trip in about an hour.
Magda: Well, it will take about an hour to get to the closest swimming area, but Marcel, our neighbor, says the best one is on the east side of the lake. Right here. He says there are fewer people, more trees, and cleaner picnic tables. There are huge rocks overlooking the water. It takes longer to get to, but it's more fun, he says.
Nazar: I guess it's worth it then. How do we get there?
Magda: It looks like we exit from Highway 36 here and drive down this road that winds around near the edge of the lake. Marcel says the swimming area is next to a restaurant, so we can eat there, if we want.
Nazar: What kind of food do they serve?
Magda: Country-style American food, like fried chicken and roast beef. Marcel says they have good prices.
Nazar: Maybe we could have dinner there in the evening, after we swim.
Magda: That would be great. We can take some snacks and drinks to have during the day and then eat dinner at the restaurant.
Nazar: Okay. I'll call Anna and James to see if they can come.

LANGUAGE SKILLS

When you are learning your way around town, you will get many ***suggestions*** about places to visit and activities that are fun. Listen carefully. These suggestions can help you choose where to go.

In this chapter you will learn two important language skills that will help you understand ***suggestions:***

- How to use describing words to paint pictures in your mind.
- How to use connecting words to show where things are located.

Using Describing Words

When someone suggests that you visit a place, they often use words that help you see it in your mind. They may talk about *colorful* gardens, *three* fountains, or *busy* sidewalks. *Colorful, three,* and *busy* are describing words.

Describing words can describe naming words or action words. This chapter will only talk about describing words with naming words.

Describing words that tell about naming words can be used in three places in a sentence.

- Before the naming word.

  Examples: The *blue* ocean pounds against the *rocky* shore.
  The *southern* breeze carried the smell of *fresh* flowers.

- After the action words **is, am, are, was, were, been, being**.

  Examples: The ocean *is blue* and the shore *is rocky.*
  The breeze *was southern*, the flowers *were fresh.*

- After the describing word **very**.
  Examples: The waves looked *very blue* against the rocks.
  The flowers smelled *very fresh* on the breeze.

TO LEARN MORE ABOUT DESCRIBING WORDS, STUDY CHAPTER 19.

Exercise 8.1

In the following sentences, underline the describing word(s) that tell something about a naming word. The first sentence has been done for you. (The answer key is on page 189.)

1. We can meet them at the parking lot.
2. Is this the right place?
3. The park has a beautiful lake.
4. The weather has been sunny for weeks.
5. You can walk on the hiking paths for hours.
6. The paths are shady and cool.
7. A good map will show us the national parks.
8. The museum is very crowded on Saturdays.
9. We live in a beautiful city.
10. The granite courthouse appeared very impressive.

Exercise 8.2

Use these describing words to complete the following sentences. In some sentences, you can use more than one word to get different meanings. The first sentence has been done for you. (The answer key is on page 189.)

beautiful	green	huge	noisy
warm	interesting	busy	soft
crowded	happy	wonderful	tall

1. The bus tour was ___wonderful___ ___crowded___ ___interesting___.
2. We saw a ______________ dinosaur.
3. The ______________ park is full of trees.
4. The ______________ restaurant had good food.
5. On a ______________ day the pool is filled with swimmers.

6. The ____________________ children run barefoot over the ____________________ grass.
7. We had a ____________________ trip to the zoo last week.
8. The shopping center is ____________________ on weekends.
9. The sky is full of ____________________ clouds.
10. We thought the lecture was very ____________________.

Using Connecting Words

Some connecting words tell where to find something. These location words help you imagine where one thing is located in relation to another.

Examples: The parking lot is *behind* the pool.
The piano is *near* the window.
Your glasses are *here* on the dining table.

Here are connecting words that show location:

near	far	next to	between
behind	in front of	across from	above
below	around	beside	outside of
inside of	under	here	there

TO LEARN MORE ABOUT CONNECTING WORDS, STUDY CHAPTER 20.

Exercise 8.3

Complete the following sentences with a connecting word that shows location. Most of the sentences have more than one right answer. The first sentence has been done for you. (The answer key is on page 189.)

1. The parking lot is between the shopping center and the movie theater.
2. Look for ____________________ the park.
3. The swimming areas are ____________________ the lake.
4. They live ____________________ away.
5. Don't they live ____________________ the gas station?
6. They could wait ____________________ the green awning.
7. The road winds ____________________ the edge of the lake.

8. Drive _______________________ the lake to the restaurant.
9. Park _______________________ the grocery store.
10. We'll meet _______________________ the movie theater.

Practice

Make up sentences that tell about where you live. Use describing words that tell color, appeal, number, shape, action, quality, and location. Use different connecting words to show where everything in your home is located in relation to other things. Also tell where your home is located in relation to other things in your neighborhood or city.

CHAPTER NINE

Visiting a Doctor/Describing

When you move to a new area, you will need to find a doctor or physician for yourself and your family. Even if you aren't sick, you may want a doctor to help you *stay* healthy. Doctors give medical exams to see if people have illnesses they don't know about. They also give shots and medicines that protect people from certain diseases.

To find a doctor, you will need to do four things:

- Decide what kind of health care you and your family need.
- Choose a doctor.
- Prepare to visit the doctor.
- Visit the doctor.

Decide what kind of health care you and your family need

There are many kinds of doctors, or physicians. Some doctors take care of general health problems. Other doctors are specialists. They take care of very specific health problems.

- *General practitioners*. General practitioners, or GPs, are sometimes called family doctors or family practitioners. These doctors can give you a general checkup. They can prescribe medicine, give shots, and take care of common health-care situations. If you have no special health problems, a GP is probably what you will need. If your doctor finds that you have a serious illness or a special problem, he or she will send you to a specialist.

USEFUL WORDS

Action words

to visit (the doctor)
to examine, to be examined
to prescribe (medicine)
to treat (an illness)
to perform (an operation)
to deliver (a baby)
to heal, to cure
to diagnose (an illness, a disease)
to take a sample (of blood, urine)
to sneeze
to cough
to run, to water
to vomit, to throw up
to run a fever, to have a fever
to faint, to pass out
to hurt, to be in pain
to poison, to be poisoned
to be allergic, to have an allergy
to be injured, to have an injury
to recover, to get well
to take (or measure) the temperature

Naming words

doctor, physician
specialist
GP, general practitioner
family practitioner
pediatrician
gynecologist, GYN
obstetrician, OB
ophthalmologist
dentist
surgeon
hospital
nurse
laboratory, lab
clinic, emergency clinic
operation, surgery
appointment
medical history
accident
AIDS
headache
cough
allergy
disease, illness
infection, bacterial infection ("bug")
virus, viral infection ("bug")
cold, flu, influenza
injury
cut, wound
bandage
fracture, broken bone
splint, cast
X-ray
crutches
temperature
blood pressure
symptom
medical examination, checkup
medicine, medication, drugs
shots, immunizations
stitches
prescription, prescription drugs
antidote (to a poison)
health insurance
health insurance company

Describing words

healthy
unwell, ill, sick
general
specific
weak, tired
nervous, jumpy
sweaty, feverish
shivery, chilled
chronic
medical
on duty
serious
mild
fatal
contagious, catching, infectious
noncontagious, noninfectious
emergency
allergic

• *Specialists.* There are many kinds of doctors who each treat patients for only one kind of problem. A dentist takes care of teeth and gums. If you decide to have a GP for most of your medical needs, you will still need a family dentist. An ophthalmologist examines eyes and prescribes glasses. If anyone in your family has eye problems, you will need an eye doctor.

Other doctors specialize in other areas of medicine. A gynecologist, also called a GYN, takes care of women's health problems. An obstetrician, also called an OB, takes care of women who are going to have babies. Usually the same doctor is both a GYN and an OB.

Shortly after the baby is born, the OB's job is done. Then the parents may take the baby either to a GP or to a children's doctor. A doctor who takes care of children is called a pediatrician.

A surgeon is a doctor who performs operations, or surgery. If your family doctor thinks that you may need an operation, he or she will send you to a surgeon.

There are many other kinds of doctors. Some take care of skin problems only—they are called dermatologists. Others treat patients with allergies—they are called allergists. Still others specialize in heart or bone diseases.

• *Clinics.* A place where many doctors work is called a clinic. Many cities have neighborhood clinics. At some clinics, you must see the doctor who is on duty at that time. Other clinics will let you choose a doctor. Some clinics provide health care for people with low incomes. You might want to call a clinic in your neighborhood to find out what it offers. (You can find the phone numbers for clinics in the yellow pages. Look under "Physicians.")

Many large cities have emergency clinics. If you have an accident or a sudden illness, you may go to an emergency clinic. These clinics can take care of things like snakebites, broken bones, burns, earaches, and vomiting. You may go to emergency clinics without an appointment.

Choose a doctor

Once you know what kinds of doctors you and your family need, you must choose a doctor. If you live in a large city, you might want to choose a doctor who has an office in your neighborhood. Or you might want one you can travel to by bus or subway.

There are many aids in finding a doctor.

• *Your job.* If you work at a place that offers health insurance, your employer may have a list of doctors who are approved by the insurance company. You must choose a doctor from this list. If your company has such a list, you may want to talk to someone you work with. Explain what you are looking for. Ask for names of good doctors from the list. If you do not have a list to choose from, you may still want to ask people at work for names of good doctors.

• *Friends and neighbors.* Friends and neighbors may help you find a doctor. A neighbor would probably know a doctor in your area. A friend from your own country might know of a doctor who speaks your native language.

• *Agencies.* Agencies, like the County Health Association, may also be able to help you. Try looking under "Health Department Services" in your phone book. If you have a social worker, ask him or her to help you. The social worker can tell you if you can get help to pay for the visit to the doctor.

Once you have the names of some doctors, check them out. You might call a doctor near you to ask if he or she can help you. You might even go talk to doctors before you choose one.

Prepare to visit the doctor

Once you have chosen a doctor, you must get ready for your first visit. If you are going to a clinic, find out if you need an appointment. Either call the clinic to find out or ask a friend.

Making an appointment. If you need to make an appointment, call the doctor's office. When you speak to the doctor's receptionist, these are the things you should talk about:

- Tell why you want to see the doctor. Explain what your medical problem is—for example, a bad cough, a pain in your side, a problem with your digestion. Perhaps you don't have a medical problem. You may just want to have a general physical exam.
- Give a *general* time when you would like to see the doctor, such as "on Wednesday," "as soon as possible," or "any morning this week." If you have an emergency and must see the doctor right away, let the receptionist know. The receptionist will make an appointment for a *specific* time that fits with your schedule.
- Say that this is your first appointment with the doctor. Ask what information you will need to give the doctor about your medical history.
- Ask about paying. You will need to know how much the doctor charges. Ask if you will need to pay when you visit or if you may pay later.

Gathering information. Once you know what information the doctor will need, either look for it in your records or try to remember it. Here are some of the things you probably will need to know:

- What diseases you and others in your family (like your parents or your brothers and sisters) have had.
- What serious injuries you have had and whether you have had any broken bones.
- What operations you have had.
- What immunization shots you have had and when you had them.
- What allergies to medicines or drugs you may have.
- What medicines you are taking now.
- The name of your health insurance company and your insurance identification number, if you have one.

Write down this information on a piece of paper before you go to your appointment, so you will have it to look at when you fill out the doctor's medical history forms.

Visit the doctor

When you get to the doctor's office, the first thing you will do is fill out your medical history forms. If you have trouble with the forms, ask the receptionist for help. The office or clinic may have someone who speaks your native language who can help you fill them out. In addition to your past medical history, these forms will ask you about the reason you want to see the doctor. If you are not feeling well, you may need to describe your symptoms.

Once the forms are filled out, you are ready to see the doctor. Sit in the waiting room until the receptionist or a nurse calls your name. A nurse will take you to an examination room, where you will wait for the doctor. The nurse will probably measure your temperature and blood pressure. He or she may ask you more questions about why you want to see the doctor—questions about your symptoms. You may have to take off your clothes and put on a special examination robe.

Don't be concerned if you must wait for 15 or 20 minutes before the doctor arrives. Doctors see many patients, and sometimes things take longer than expected. However, you should not have to wait longer than 30 minutes. If you have been waiting that long, ask a nurse about the delay. You may decide to wait longer, or you may decide to make another appointment for a different day.

FINDING A DOCTOR: A SAMPLE CONVERSATION

Su Li Wong wants to take her children to the doctor. Her five-year-old child will be starting school soon. He needs a checkup. She also has a three-year-old who has been sneezing a lot lately. She has decided to talk to Mary, her neighbor, about going to the doctor.

Su Li: Hello, Mary. Do you have time to talk?
Mary: Sure! Come in, Su Li. Have a cup of tea with me.
Su Li: Thank you. While we are drinking our tea, can we talk about doctors?

Mary: I was just thinking about doctors myself. Bobby and Sally will be going back to school next week. I have to take them to their pediatrician for shots. Do you have a pediatrician?
Su Li: Not yet, but someone has recommended Dr. Keller. My Li Pung is starting school. I want him to go to the doctor first. Do you know what the doctor will do? I want to tell Li Pung what will happen so he will not be afraid.
Mary: First, the doctor will weigh and measure him. Li Pung may need shots. Did you get a form from the school? It tells what he needs.
Su Li: Yes, I filled out most of the form easily. But I could use some help.
Mary: What's the problem?
Su Li: There is a word I don't know. Will you help me?
Mary: What's the word?
Su Li: I do not know what "immunizations" are. The form asks if my child has had immunization for measles.
Mary: Immunizations are the shots I was talking about. Children must have them to keep from getting childhood diseases. Do you know what shots Li Pung has had?
Su Li: Yes, when he was a baby, he had all the necessary shots. Then he had more last year. I have a list of all of them.
Mary: That's good. You can take the list with you to the doctor in case you can't remember all the names of the shots.
Su Li: Do I need to take him to a special doctor for his eyes?
Mary: Doctors come to the schools to test the children's eyes and hearing. If they tell you Li Pung has problems, you will need to take him to an eye specialist.
Su Li: Oh, thank you so much, Mary. Do you mind if I use your phone? I will call Dr. Keller's office now to make an appointment.

VISITING THE DOCTOR: A SAMPLE CONVERSATION

Su Li has arrived at the doctor's office with her two children. Li Pung has been examined for school. Now Su Li must talk to the doctor about her younger child, Young, who has been sneezing a lot.
Su Li: Thank you, Doctor, for checking Li Pung. I am glad he has had all his shots.
Doctor: Li Pung is a healthy little boy.
Su Li: Do you have time to look at Young also?
Doctor: Does she have a problem?
Su Li: For several days she has been sneezing. Her eyes water, too. But she does not cough, so I do not think she has a cold. Do you think the problem is serious?
Doctor: She may have an allergy. Allergies are very common in this area. The end of summer is a common time for allergies. She may be allergic to some flowers.
Su Li: Is there a way to find out what she is allergic to? Is there medicine she can take?
Doctor: First, I will check her to see if she has a cold. If that is not the problem, I will give her an allergy test. The test will have to go to the lab. Can you call me in a few days? I will know then what the test shows. If Young has an allergy, I will call your drugstore with a prescription for medicine. Do you know if your insurance covers the cost of medicine?
Su Li: I will check the insurance policy.

The doctor examines Young and sends the tests to the lab. In a few days, she calls Su Li.
Doctor: Hello, Mrs. Wong. This is Dr. Keller. If have good news for you. Young is a healthy child. She does have a slight allergy to some flowers and trees.
Su Li: Thank you very much for calling, Doctor. I am glad there is nothing seriously wrong with Young. Did you call the drugstore with the prescription?
Doctor: Yes, it's all taken care of.
Su Li: I will pick up the medicine today. Our insurance covers the cost of most medicine. I looked at the policy yesterday. It covers medicine for allergies.
Doctor: Follow the directions on the bottle. She must take the medicine three times a day. Please call in two days to let me know how she is. If she has any problems with the medicine, call me immediately.
Su Li: Thank you very much, Doctor. It is good to know there is nothing seriously wrong.

Doctor: Goodbye, Mrs. Wong.
Su Li: Goodbye, Dr. Keller. I will let you know how Young is doing.

LANGUAGE SKILLS

When you visit a doctor, you must ***ask*** and ***answer*** questions. You must ask questions about the *present* and the *future*. You must answer questions about the *present* and the *past*. When you answer questions, often you must describe how or when something happened.

In this chapter, you will learn two important language skills for ***asking*** and ***answering*** questions:

- How to ask questions.
- How to describe *how* or *when* something happened.

Using Asking Sentences

One way to ask questions is to use asking words, like **who, what,** and **when**. Another way to ask questions is to begin your sentence with a helping word or action word. Here are a few common helping or action words you will use often to ask questions.

Helping/action words	***Examples***
to be: am, is, are, was, were, will be	*Am* I on time?
	Is she here?
	Are they doctors?
	Was the doctor clear?
	Were the children sick?
	Will you *be* here tomorrow?
to do: do, does, did, will do	*Do* you know the doctor?
	Does he like children?
	Did you make an appointment?
	Will the doctor *do* the tests?
to have: has, have, will have	*Has* the doctor called yet?
	Have you seen the doctor?
	Will you *have* an operation?

Here are the two ways you can build questions that begin with an action word or a helping word:

- Helping/action word + naming word + action word
  Do *you* *cough?*
- Helping/action word + naming word + naming or describing word
  Is *she* *a doctor?*

TO LEARN MORE ABOUT ASKING SENTENCES, STUDY CHAPTER 21.

Exercise 9.1

Here are some sentences about visiting the doctor. Each sentence is the answer to a question. In the space after each sentence, write a question to go with the answer. Begin your question with the action word or helping word that is written before the space. The first question has been done for you. (The answer key is on page 189.)

1. Su Li visited the doctor.
   Did ______ Su Li visit the doctor? ______
2. Su Li's daughter needs medicine.
   Does ______
3. You have the firm with you.
   Do ______
4. The doctor is ready to see me.
   Is ______
5. She has finished the checkup.
   Has ______
6. You have questions for the doctor.
   Do ______
7. The doctor was in.
   Was ______
8. You have taken your medicine.
   Have ______
9. She is taking medicine.
   Is ______
10. They are here to see the doctor.
   Are ______

Using Describing Words

English has many words to describe. One kind of describing word ends in **-ly**. Describing words that end in **-ly** mean one of two things:

- In a certain way (how).

  Examples: The doctor examined the child *carefully*.
  The doctor works *quickly* in an emergency.
  I sleep *badly* unless my back is supported.

- At a certain time (when).

  Examples: I visited the doctor *recently*.
  If she has trouble breathing, call the doctor *immediately*.
  The children have a medical checkup *yearly*.

TO LEARN MORE ABOUT DESCRIBING WORDS, STUDY CHAPTER 19.

Exercise 9.2

Underline the describing words in the following sentences that tell *how* or *when* something happens, will happen, or has happened. Then put an "H" in the space if the word tells *how* or a "W" if it tells *when*. The first sentence has been done for you. (The answer key is on page 189.)

H 1. Mary gladly explained the meaning of "immunization" to Su Li.

_ 2. Su Li quickly called for an appointment with Dr. Keller.

_ 3. Dr. Keller examined Li Pung thoroughly.

_ 4. She confidently said Li Pung was a healthy little boy.

_ 5. Then Dr. Keller gently examined Young.

_ 6. Su Li was slightly worried about Young's sneezing.

_ 7. Dr. Keller calmly explained that Young had allergies.

_ 8. She told Su Li to give Young three allergy pills daily.

_ 9. Young will feel better immediately.

_ 10. Gradually, she may outgrow her allergies.

Practice

Make up questions you can ask when:

- Calling for an appointment with a doctor.
- Seeing a doctor about a medical problem.

Begin your questions with an *action word* or a *helping word*.

Make up sentences that talk about your health. Be sure to make up some sentences that tell *how* or *when* something happens or has happened.

CHAPTER TEN

Talking to Your Landlord/Complaining

When you rent from a landlord, you have some responsibilities to your landlord. Your landlord also has responsibilities to you. When you move into a new home, you must do the following things:

- Know everyone's responsibilities.
- Check your new home before you move in.
- Learn how to talk to the landlord when a problem arises.

Know everyone's responsibilities

When you rent a house or an apartment, you most likely will have a lease that talks about your responsibilities and your landlord's responsibilities. Most landlords use a standard lease form, but some do not. If you do have a lease, know what it says. Sometimes the language in a lease is very hard to understand. If you can't read it, get someone to explain it to you.

Know your responsibilities. Different kinds of leases will describe different responsibilities you might have. For example, you might be expected to tell your landlord if you have a visitor in your home for longer than a week. Or you might be expected to keep your pets outdoors at all times. But there are certain things that everyone must do as a renter:

- Pay your rent on time.
- Do not disturb your neighbors.
- Keep the property clean.
- Let the landlord know what needs to be fixed.
- Give your landlord plenty of notice when you want to move out.

If you do not keep up with the rent, the landlord can ask you to leave. If you pay your rent late, the landlord may charge you a late fee. If the property gets run down because you do not

USEFUL WORDS

Action words	Naming words	Describing words
to maintain (in good repair, condition)	landlord	damaged, broken
to repair, to fix	renter, tenant	normal
to replace	responsibility	careless
to complain	lease, rental agreement	unsafe, dangerous
to leak	property	shabby, worn
to short out	fee, charge	spotted, stained
to break, to damage	appliances	fresh, new
to clog, to be clogged	plumbing	rusty, corroded
to stop up, to back up	stain, spot	
	electrical outlet, wall socket, plug	
	faucet	
	toilet	
	maintenance man, superintendent ("super")	
	temperature	
	thermostat	
	electrical switch, wall switch	
	wiring	
	complaint	
	passkey	

take proper care, the landlord can charge you for repairs. For example, if your children break something, you may have to pay for it. If you are careless and spill things on the carpets, you may have to pay for the cleaning.

Know your landlord's responsibilities. Your landlord has responsibilities, too. The landlord must:

- Respect your privacy.
- See that the property is properly maintained.
- Talk to other tenants if they are disturbing you.
- Give you plenty of notice if he wants you to move out.

If appliances break down, it is the landlord's responsibility to have them fixed. If the landlord has agreed to paint the apartment, to wash the windows, to keep the lawn trimmed and weeded, and to keep the carpets clean, he must do so.

It is important to know what you must do and what the landlord must do. If you do not have a lease, talk to the landlord before you move in. Think about what is important to you about your home. Then ask any questions that you have. Be sure you know what the landlord is willing to do. Write down everything he promises. Also write down anything you have agreed to do.

Check your new home before you move in

Before you move into your apartment or house, you and your landlord together should fill out a checklist that describes the condition of your new home. This checklist tells you and your landlord two things:

A SAMPLE AGREEMENT

Landlord agrees to:
- Get paint for the apartment.
- Clean the carpets every two years.
- See that all appliances work.
- Pay for any plumbing repairs.
- Pay for any heating repairs.
- Mow the lawn and trim the shrubs.
- Have the outsides of the windows washed every spring.

Tenant agrees to:
- Paint the apartment with the paint the landlord buys.
- Keep the sidewalks clear of snow.
- Keep the insides of the windows clean.

- Repairs and improvements that must be made before you move in (or very soon after you move in).
- Any *new* damage that you will be responsible for when you move out.

On this checklist, you should describe *everything* you see. You might notice that there is a stain on the carpet, that the kitchen cabinets have been scratched, that the bedroom wall behind the door has a small hole in it. These are things that you should *not* be responsible for when you are ready to move out.

If you find problems during this check, talk it over right away with your landlord.

Later on, after you have lived in your home for a while, new problems may come up. If you have a problem with the property, let the landlord know right away. Maybe your bathroom faucet will start to leak. Your refrigerator may break down or your closet shelf may begin to sag. Make a list of all the things that need to be done. Date the list. Be sure to ask your landlord *when* he will take care of the problem. Do this every time you ask the landlord to do something for the apartment or house.

Learn how to talk to the landlord when a problem arises

When there is a problem in your home and you must talk to the landlord, keep in mind these simple rules:

- *Be polite.* Greet your landlord in a friendly manner. Speak in a regular, quiet voice.
- *Be clear.* The landlord must know what is wrong before he can help you. If you do not know the name of the appliance that is broken, find out. Ask a friend. If you do not think the landlord will understand you, take someone along to help you. Explain to the landlord that your friend will help you with your English.
- *Be organized.* The landlord is a busy person. You are a busy person, too. Take some time to decide exactly what you want to tell him. Before you go to see the landlord, make a list of all the things you want him to do.
- *Be cooperative.* Call your landlord ahead of time to let him know you want to come and talk to him. Set a time that is good for both of you. When you talk to him, realize that it sometimes takes a while to find a workman. Do not demand that the problem be taken care of immediately. Let the landlord know when it would be convenient for you to let the workman in. (The landlord might be willing to use his passkey to let the workman in if you cannot be home. If you need the landlord's help, ask politely. Do not say, "You'll have to let the plumber in. I won't be home.")
- *Know your rights.* Keep copies of your lease and your lists. If necessary, remind your landlord of his promises. Don't say, "I think . . ." Say, "I remember . . ." or "The lease says . . ." or "My list shows . . ."

• *Be firm.* Do not let the landlord take advantage of you. If you are sure it is your right to have something fixed, do not let the landlord ignore you. If necessary, remind him that he promised to make certain repairs.

• *Ask questions.* If you are not sure what the landlord is promising, ask questions. Be sure you get clear answers. Know what work is going to be done, when, and by whom.

If you have done everything listed above and you still have problems, there is one more way you might be able to get your problems solved. Many cities have a Renters' Association. If your landlord has not done something that you are *sure* is his responsibility, you can complain to this group. (Look in the phone book to find the phone number of this group in your city.) If there is no such group in your city, talk to other tenants of your landlord. Ask them if they have problems like yours. If they do, organize into a formal tenants' group. Arrange to talk to the landlord together about your problems. You will all have more power to get what you need if you act as a group.

SAMPLE CHECKLIST

Living Room

Objects	**Condition**	**Work to be done**
carpets	spotted	will be cleaned
drapes	new	none
walls	marked	will be painted
windows	clean	none
outlets	working	none

Kitchen

Objects	**Condition**	**Work to be done**
dishwasher	working	none
stove	clean, working	none
faucets	no leaks	none
floor	needs new tile	will be replaced
counters	stained	will not be repaired
refrigerator	icemaker broken	will not be fixed

Bedroom

Objects	**Condition**	**Work to be done**
walls	dirty	will be painted
drapes	no drapes	tenant must supply
tile	clean, polished	none
outlets	working	none
window	lock missing	will be replaced
shelves in closet	none	will be added

Bathroom

Objects	**Condition**	**Work to be done**
shower	working	none
faucets	rusty	will not be replaced
toilet	working	none
outlets	working	none

TALKING TO A NEIGHBOR: A SAMPLE CONVERSATION

Maria Garcia and her family just moved into the Creekside Apartments. She has been checking over the apartment and making a list for her landlord of things that need to be done. As she finishes her list, her doorbell rings.

Sally: Hi, I'm Sally Carter! I live in apartment 324, right next door. I was wondering if you could do a favor for me. I'm expecting a package to be delivered, but I have to go talk to the landlord. Could you sign for the package and hold it for me?

Maria: Of course. I would be happy to help you out. By the way, my name is Maria Garcia. We have just moved in here—myself, my husband Raúl, and our two kids. It is nice to meet you.

Sally: Joe and I have lived here for six months. Joe is my husband.

Maria: Would you like to come in for a cup of coffee?

Sally: Thanks, Maria. I can only stay a few minutes. I need to talk to the landlord about some problems with my apartment.

Maria: What trouble are you having, Sally?

Sally: My oven gets too hot. I baked a cake yesterday. After only thirty minutes, the cake was as hard as a brick! I had the temperature set right. The cake shouldn't have cooked that fast. There must be something wrong with the thermostat in my oven. He'll have to get it repaired.

Maria: I have been having trouble with my electricity. When I plug the vacuum cleaner into the socket in the living room, the vacuum doesn't turn on.

Sally: There may be something wrong with the wiring. That is unsafe. You should talk to the landlord, too.

Maria: I was just making a list of things, but I must stay here now. The children will be home from school soon. And besides, I must sign for your package when it is delivered.

Sally: I really appreciate that, Maria. I'm sure glad that you moved in next door to me. Hey, I'll bake you a cake as a housewarming gift—as soon as my oven is working! (They laugh.)

Maria: That sounds great. Well, I'll see you later.

Sally: Bye for now.

TALKING TO YOUR LANDLORD: A SAMPLE CONVERSATION

The next morning, Maria calls the landlord to arrange a meeting time. They agree to meet in his office.

Juan: Good morning, Maria. How do you and Raúl like your new apartment?

Maria: We like many things about living here. My children have friends to play with and a safe playground here. I am planning to start a job soon, and I understand that a woman upstairs watches many of the children after school. That is all wonderful. But there a few things I want to talk to you about.

Juan: What do you need?

Maria: Since I will be starting to work away from home, I want to have all the maintenance for the apartment done first. Before we moved in, you said we could choose a paint color for the children's room. The children want the room painted yellow.

Juan: We have painters coming next week to paint rooms in three apartments. I will put your name on the list. Wednesday morning is free. Would that be a good time for you?

Maria: Yes, that would be a good time. I don't start my job until the week after next.

Juan: I will give you some paint samples. The children can choose from three different shades of yellow.

Maria: Thank you. They like choosing how their room will look. There are a few other things that need to be taken care of. You promised to have some shelves put in the children's closet. When can that be done?

Juan: Our maintenance man can take care of that. Bill is free on Friday morning. Will that be a good time for you?

Maria: I have a doctor's appointment at 8 A.M. Can Bill come after 10?

Juan: Yes, he will be free then. I'll fill out a work order for you. How many shelves to you want?

Maria: The shelves need to be eighteen inches apart so the children have room to put toys on them. I have measured the space. There is room for three more shelves below the one that is already there.

Juan: Fine. Consider it done! Is there anything else?

Maria: Yes. The electrical outlet in the living room doesn't seem to be working right. I am afraid bad wiring could cause a fire.
Juan: Did you know that there is a wall switch that controls that outlet? The switch must be turned on to bring electricity to that outlet. You can plug a lamp into the outlet and turn it on at the door as you come in.
Maria: No, I did not think of that. I'll check the switch. There may not be a problem with the electricity after all. Well, thanks for your help. I'll show the paint samples to the children when they get home. Carlos and José can return them later. Will you be home at 5 P.M.?
Juan: Yes, that is a good time for me. Thank you for coming over. I like to keep my tenants happy. If you do your part, I will do mine.
Maria: Thank you. I will call you to let you know about the switch. Goodbye.
Juan: Goodbye, Maria.

LANGUAGE SKILLS

When talking to your landlord, you may have to make some ***complaints***. Complaints often tell about what has happened in the past and what will happen in the future. In this chapter, you will learn this important language skill for ***expressing complaints:***

- How to use connecting words to show the relation between things that happen at different times.

Using Connecting Words

The following words help tell when something *happens, has happened,* or *will happen:*

when	whenever	while	after
before	as	until	since
ever since	as soon as	once	as long as

These words help us to put two ideas into one sentence. They help us to see which of two actions in the sentence happened first, or if they happened at the same time.

Example: The landlord was nice. I asked him a question.
The landlord was nice *when* I ask him a question.

Sometimes these words come in the middle of a sentence.

Examples: The workman will finish *as soon as* he can.
The carpenter will work *until* the job is done.
The painter has worked *since* he was sixteen.
He has had the same job *ever since* 1978.
He never stops working *once* he starts.
The landlord will help *as long as* there are problems.

Sometimes these words come at the beginning of a sentence.

Examples: *When* I finish, I will help you.
Whenever I paint, I get paint in my hair.
While the children are gone, I will paint their room.
After I finish painting, I clean the brushes.
Before the children get home, I will put the furniture back in place.
Until I talk to the maintenance man, I cannot schedule the work.
Once the work is done, I'll be happy.

TO LEARN MORE ABOUT CONNECTING WORDS, STUDY CHAPTER 20.

Exercise 10.1

Underline the word that best completes the sentence. The first sentence has been done for you. (The answer key is on page 189.)

1. **[As] [<u>After</u>]** I finish the painting, I'll eat lunch.
2. **[When] [Until]** the children are in school, I can get a lot of work done.
3. **[While] [After]** my neighbor leaves, I'll talk to the painters.
4. **[As soon as] [Since]** I finish, I'll go home.
5. **[Ever since] [Until]** we moved here, we have had trouble.
6. **[Once] [Until]** the furnace is fixed, we will be warm.
7. We will be cold in January, **[as long as] [ever since]** the heat is off.
8. We must stop painting **[whenever] [after]** it rains.
9. **[Before] [Until]** the house falls down, we must have some work done.
10. The painters will work **[until] [as]** it is too dark to see.

Practice

Make up sentences that express a complaint you have about something in your life right now—maybe about something that is wrong with your apartment or house. Try putting some of your sentences together by using the connecting words *when, whenever, while, after, before, as, until, since, ever since, as soon as, once, as long as*.

CHAPTER ELEVEN

Talking to Your Boss and Co-workers/Problem Solving

To do your job well, you must know how to work with your boss and your co-workers. Clear communication is an especially important part of working together. Here are the three most important things you must do when you talk to your boss and co-workers:

- Listen to instructions.
- Cooperate with others.
- Discuss work matters.

Listen to instructions

Listening is an important skill to learn. You will know what you are supposed to do only if you listen clearly. Here are three steps to follow:

- *Pay attention to the person who is speaking*. When someone is talking to you, *look* at him or her. Also look closely at anything he or she is showing to you while talking. And keep your mind on what the speaker is saying. Don't think about something else, even if it is on the same subject.
- *Ask questions*. If you hear something that you don't understand, be sure to ask about it. Maybe you just didn't *hear* a word or two: "Did you say I should get the *bench* or the *wrench*?" Maybe you didn't *understand* the meaning of a word or sentence: "What does 'bottom line' mean?" Maybe you understood what was said, but need to know more about it. For example, your boss may tell you to do a certain piece of work by a certain time. You might want him to explain *how* to do the work, *why* the work needs to be done, or *what* to do if you finish early. Ask your questions clearly, so your boss will know what to tell you. And if you still don't understand, ask again. Don't worry about looking bad to your boss. He wants you to have a good understanding of his instructions.
- *Repeat what you heard*. This is a good way to check that you heard everything correctly. Just say the instructions back to the person who gave them to you. If you have missed anything

USEFUL WORDS

Action words	Naming words	Describing words
to plan, to make plans	supervisor	efficient
to organize	leadman	inefficient
to control	subordinate, worker	effective
to delegate (work, tasks)	manager	ineffective
to manage	chain of command	productive
to supervise	workplace	nonproductive
to perform, to do	control	quality (high/good, low/poor)
to analyze, to study	quality control	on time, on schedule
to solve (problems), to problem-solve	schedule	overdue, late
to cooperate	cooperation	cooperative
to instruct, to give instructions	productivity	monthly
to order, to give orders	teamwork	quarterly
to expedite	skills	annually
to train, to give training	experience	
to pay attention	work flow	
to evaluate	slowdown	
to motivate	error, mistake, flaw	
to reward	shift, work shift	
	quota	
	production	
	authority	
	responsibility	
	opinion, point of view	
	incentive, motivation	
	evaluation	
	performance	
	input	
	feedback	
	bottom line	
	meeting, conference	
	agenda	
	grievance	
	department	
	division	
	work unit, work group, work team	
	memo, memorandum	

important, your boss will know and give you the instructions again.

These three steps to listening also work in other situations—for example, when your boss is giving you feedback on your work. Feedback is how you learn what you have been doing well and what you need to do better. If you pay attention, ask questions, and repeat what you have heard, you will understand what your boss likes and does not like.

Cooperate with others

Your company depends upon everyone who works there. Even a job that seems small or unimportant is needed in the company. Because everyone is going a job that the company needs to be done, cooperation between workers is important. Good teamwork depends on getting along with one another. Here are some tips for cooperation when you have a disagreement with a co-worker or your boss:

- *Talk it over.* You must do two things when talking over a disagreement: (1) try to explain your "side" of the situation (*your reasons*) and (2) try to understand the other person's "side" of the situation (*their reasons*). Often, people who disagree just don't know all the facts. When they learn the reasons *why* their co-worker said or did a certain thing, they begin to see the whole situation instead of just their "side" of it.

  Of course, there are times when a disagreement is caused by more than not knowing all the facts. Sometimes people know the same facts but have very different *opinions* about those facts. By talking it over, they may be able to shorten the distance between their two different points of view.

- *Put your work responsibilities first.* Personal disagreements should not prevent you from doing your job. If you disagree with one of your co-workers or your boss—or even strongly *dislike* him—it must not stop you from doing the best job that you can do. Sometimes you may have to keep your opinion to yourself so everyone can get along together. Sometimes you may have to do tasks that are unpleasant or inconvenient for you so others can have what they need to do *their* jobs. Sometimes you may have to ask for information, advice, or help in solving a problem from someone you don't like.

- *Put the past behind you.* If you have a disagreement with someone at work, don't let it go on and on. When the situation is over, do not hold on to any feelings of anger or doubt toward your co-worker. Show that you are ready to be at peace with him or her. Remember that disagreements are a natural part of life in a company, and that they can be settled and left behind.

Discuss work matters

You must discuss work matters every day with your boss and co-workers—to make plans, solve problems, and move the work along smoothly. Here are four matters you probably will have to discuss:

- *Dividing work tasks.* Usually everyone in a work group knows what their tasks are. But sometimes the supervisor must divide work tasks among his or her workers. Maybe a special project must be done. Or perhaps the responsibilities of the whole work group have been changed. At these times, you should talk about what you and your co-workers each must do. Everyone must know exactly what his or her responsibilities are—so that some tasks don't get done *twice* while other tasks are not done *at all*.

- *Making schedules.* Schedules help get work done on time. They tell how long each part of the work should take. They also tell the order in which tasks must be done. And, of course, they tell when *everything* must be finished. When you talk to your boss and co-workers about schedules, you must know which part of the work you are responsible for. You also must know if another worker must do *his* part before you can do *yours*. Then you can talk to that worker about timing your work.

- *Setting quality standards.* Sometimes you must talk to your boss and co-workers about how to measure if a job has been done well. Your boss may want to give you feedback on the quality of your work. Or you and your co-workers may want to give each other feedback on how your work group is doing. Talking about quality standards helps everyone do a better job. Quality can be measured in several different ways—by speed (how fast do you work?), by numbers (how many things can you finish?), by perfection (how few mistakes do you make?). When you are just learning how to do a task, the quality of your work will not be so good. Later,

HOW TO FIT INTO YOUR COMPANY

When you start to work for a company, you must learn many things. Of course, you must learn your *job*. But you must also learn how to *fit into* your company. Every company is like a small country—with its own customs, history, and government. When you go to work for a company, you must learn to become a "citizen" of that company.

Customs. Your company probably has customs about:

- How to dress for work.
- When to take breaks and how long breaks should last.
- When and where to eat and drink.
- How long you can be away from your place.
- How neat your place must be.
- How you may decorate your place.
- Whose opinion is most important.
- What personal information you may share (or not share).
- What you can complain about (and what you can't).
- Even what kind of jokes are funny!

Watch and listen to your co-workers so you can learn about the customs in your company. You will feel much more "at home" when you can follow these company customs.

History. Every company has stories about its past. There are stories about the company itself. And there are stories about people who work (or used to work) for the company. Your company has stories about:

- The opinions and interests of top managers.
- The work the top managers did in the past.
- Big mistakes in the company.
- Big successes in the company.
- The people who caused big changes in the company.

You can learn your company's history from your co-workers. These stories can help you understand *why* the company does things in the particular way it does.

Government. Every company is organized in two directions: (1) up-down and (2) side-side. *Up-down* has to do with power and authority. For example, the company president has a great deal of power and authority, a manager has less, and a supervisor has even less. This is called the chain of command. *Side-side* has to do with different kinds of jobs that must be done. For example, one department is in charge of making things, another is in charge of selling them, and a third is in charge of getting the money when they are sold.

Learn about your company's government from your boss and your co-workers. This information will help you know how your company works.

your quality should get better and better.

- *Coordinating efforts.* You may have a job that you do on your own. Or you may have a job that involves doing tasks with your co-workers. When you work together with others, you must coordinate your efforts. That means you must share information, discuss problems, make plans, ask questions, and get along with each other. It is best to talk openly to people you work with in this way. All of you will feel more satisfaction and less frustration. And you will do a better job.

TALKING TO CO-WORKERS: A SAMPLE CONVERSATION

Manuel Gomez is a supervisor at the Diaz Hardware Company, a small factory that makes different kinds of nuts and bolts. He supervises workers who check the hardware for cracks and other flaws. Every month, Manuel meets with his work group to discuss issues of concern about their work and company policies. This month they are talking about benefits.

Manuel: It's time to talk about benefits. Does

anyone have a concern?
Rosita: I am concerned about day care for my children. I must drive ten miles across town to take my children to a day-care center. If they get sick, I must drive back to get them. I lose working time and pay. I would like to see the company do something about day care.
Angela: Not all of us have children. I don't. I care about Rosita's problem, because she is my friend. But I don't want all the company benefits to go to other people. Those who don't need day care shouldn't have to pay for it.
Ming: I am concerned about day care, but I am also concerned about working conditions.

No one else mentions any concerns. They all agree to discuss these topics.
Manuel: Since Rosita mentioned day care first, let's start with that.
Rosita: I have a suggestion about day care that will not cost much. There is empty space in the building. I know of someone who wants to open a day-care service. Maybe the boss would rent her space. Then we could bring the children to work with us. Those of us who want to use the service could pay for it. It would be convenient to have our children nearby.
Mousa: This sounds like a good possibility. It would benefit people who need day care, but it wouldn't cost the company money. Those who do not need day care would not be receiving a useless benefit.
Manuel: Well, this is something that I need to talk about with the other supervisors. We'll see how many other employees are interested in day care. If the number is large enough, I think the boss will consider it. . . . Who else wants to talk? Ming, didn't you mention working conditions?
Ming: My eyes aren't as good as they once were. I'm worried that I might not be finding all of the bad nuts and bolts when I make my inspections. I would like brighter lighting so I can see better.
Rosita: Yes, I think it needs to be brighter in our work area, too. I sometimes get headaches.
Manuel: I agree that is an important point. I'll talk to the boss about that right away. Is there

HOW TO BE A RESPONSIBLE EMPLOYEE

Working in this country may be very different from working in your native country. In this country, employers expect and like things in their employees that the employers in your country may not expect or like. You must learn what these differences are, so you can do your work to the best of your ability.

- If you see a problem—or a *possible* problem—speak up. Don't wait for someone else to point it out. No one may notice it but *you*.
- If you see something that needs to be done, offer to do it. Don't wait for your boss to ask you to do it. He has many things to take care of and counts on you to share this responsibility.
- If you see a way to do something better or faster, tell your boss. Before you try your idea, check with him first—sometimes a good idea can have bad results in some other part of the company. But be sure to tell him about your idea instead of keeping it to yourself. Even if the idea isn't as good as you thought at first, your boss will be glad that you are trying to make things better.
- If you are not busy, offer to help someone else. But be sure you have done your own work first. Of course, if your boss asks you to help someone else, then do it right away—even if your work is not done.
- If you don't understand something, ask about it. Keep asking until it is clear to you. Most bosses prefer to answer a hundred small questions rather than fix one big mistake.
- If you make a mistake, learn from it. Pay attention to how you made the mistake, so you don't accidentally make it again.

Of course, it is also a good idea to try to learn new things even when you *haven't* made a mistake. Learn from watching and listening to your co-workers. Ask your boss to let you try new tasks and learn about new machines. He will see that you want to be a valuable employee.

any more input? No? All right. I will talk to the other supervisors about day care. And I will talk to the boss about the lighting. You have had good suggestions. I am sure we can work these things out. I know you all want to head for home now. I'll see you all tomorrow. Goodbye!

TALKING TO YOUR BOSS: A SAMPLE CONVERSATION

Manuel is now meeting with the company's owner and manager, Sylvia Diaz. They meet monthly to talk about his workers' needs and problems. He is telling her about a proposal he has and about the recent meeting with his work group.

Sylvia: Hello, Manuel. It's good to see that you are right on time as usual! Come in and sit down.

Manuel: Good afternoon, Sylvia. I wanted to be on time since we have so much to talk about today.

Sylvia: Yes, I see we are scheduled to talk about wages and benefits.

Manuel: It's that time of year again!

Sylvia: What specific items do you want to discuss?

Manuel: Let's talk about wages first. You know there is a new government minimum wage law going into effect. Since this is a small company, the law doesn't require us to follow the minimum wage scale. Our starting wages have been just under the current minimum wage level. But I suggest that you increase starting wages to meet the new minimum wage law. That way, we can attract the most reliable workers.

Sylvia: Yes, I agree. If we get the Ace contract, we'll need to increase our production by about 50 percent. That means we'll need to hire about a dozen new people. I want to get good workers who will stay with the company.

Manuel: Good. Now I have a suggestion from one of my workers about day care. It is an idea that will not cost the company much money.

Sylvia: I know that many of our workers need good day care. I would like to hear this idea.

Manuel: Rosita knows someone who would like to open a day-care service. There is also empty space in the building. We thought that you might be willing to rent the space to Rosita's friend. This should be very convenient for anyone who wants to have their children nearby.

Sylvia: Hmm. That is an interesting proposal. I think that you should get some feedback from the other supervisors. They can see if their workers would also like this day-care service. Send me a memo on their reactions, and I will make a final decision.

Manuel: There is one other concern that was raised at our group meeting. Everyone feels that they need better lighting to do their work well.

Sylvia: That is an important point. The workers should certainly be able to see properly to do their work. I agree that this needs to be taken care of.

Manuel: Thank you. I will let my group know about this.

Sylvia: Thanks for your input, Manuel. And I will be thinking about the day-care proposal.

LANGUAGE SKILLS

When you are talking with your boss or coworkers, you often are trying to ***solve problems***. Usually, when you talk about the solutions to problems, you use the word *should*. You talk about what someone *should* do—the boss, the workers, the supplier, the customer. You also talk about what people *should not* do. In this chapter, you will learn three important language skills for ***solving problems***:

- How to use the helping word *should* with action words.
- How to use the connecting word *that* to join two parts of one sentence.
- How to substitute general naming words for particular naming words.

Using Helping Words

English has a number of words that are used to *help* action words. These words are **would, can, could, shall, should, may, might,** and **must.**

Examples: The crew *can* finish the project in one week.
We *must* finish the project tomorrow.
I *would* like to have a little more time.

In this chapter, we will focus on the helping word **should**. This word is useful when you want to talk about things that are necessary or required.

- **Should** has two different meanings:
  - Sometimes it means *ought to*.

    Examples: We *should* ask the boss what she thinks about this.
    The boxes *should* be stacked along the wall.
  - Sometimes it means *will*.

    Examples: We *should* get an answer before tomorrow.
    Mousa *should* have the boxes stacked by noon.

- When the word **not** follows the helping word **should**, the meaning is the same as *ought not to*.

  Examples: We *should not* leave early.

  We *should not* complain without reason.

- The words **should** and **should not** do not change, no matter how many people are doing the action.

  Examples: *I should not* help him until I'm finished here.
  We should work quickly so we can leave early.
  You should not start working this late.
  She should get some help with that project.
  They should not go home before quitting time.

- **Should** and **should not** can be used to ask questions. (When we ask a question we usually say **shouldn't** rather than **should not**.)

  Examples: *Should* we be paid for overtime?
  Shouldn't he earn more money for more work?

TO LEARN MORE ABOUT USING HELPING WORDS WITH ACTION WORDS, STUDY CHAPTER 18.

Exercise 11.1

Here is a conversation between two co-workers. If a sentence tells what *will* happen, mark it with a "W." If a sentence tells what *ought to* happen, mark it with an "O." The first answer has been done for you. (The answer key is on page 189.)

1. ***Ming:*** I should get a raise next month, since I've worked here a year. <u>W</u>
2. ***Rosita:*** I should get one, too, because I work so hard! ___
3. ***Ming:*** Should we go to lunch now? Is it noon? ___
4. ***Rosita:*** Almost. It should take us just a few minutes to finish up here. ___

5. ***Ming:*** I should go right home at five o'clock, but I plan to work late. ___
6. ***Rosita:*** Well, I should stop at the store, but I will be too tired. ___
7. ***Ming:*** What are you going to eat? I should get a salad. ___
8. ***Rosita:*** We should both eat salads, but I want a piece of pie! ___
9. ***Ming:*** I ate too much pie yesterday and lost my appetite for sweets. I should get it back by tomorrow, though!___
10. ***Rosita:*** I should get back to work now. My lunch break is over. ___
11. ***Ming:*** See you later. I need to talk to Manuel about the new lighting. He should be in his office. ___

Using Connecting Words

Connecting words link one part of a sentence with another part. There are many kinds of connecting words. One useful connecting word is the word **that**. The word **that** may be used after these special action words:

say	believe	think	decide	see
agree	propose	prove	suggest	assume
demand	wish	hope	confess	recommend

That is used to connect one naming word/action word set with another naming word/action word set. Look at the two sets of words connected by **that** in these sentences:

Examples: He said *that* he would talk to the manager.
He said + he would talk
The group decided *that* we would ask for a raise.
The group decided + we would ask
I think *that* Bob should get the promotion.
I think + Bob should get

TO LEARN MORE ABOUT CONNECTING WORDS, STUDY CHAPTER 20.

Exercise 11.2

Write a special action word in the space in the following sentences. Try to use a different special action word from the list for each sentence. The first one has been done for you. (The answer key is on page 190.)

1. Manuel __proposed__ that we get paid according to our production.
2. We ____________ that we wanted to have day care.
3. Ming ____________ that she will work better if the lighting is brighter.
4. We ____________ that Manuel should talk to the other supervisors.
5. I ____________ that we could come to work later and leave earlier.
6. Angela ____________ that she wasn't interested in day care.

Using Naming Words

There are two kinds of naming words: particular naming words and substitute naming words. *Particular* naming words give the actual name of someone, someplace, or something. For example: Imad, New York, newspaper, door. *Substitute* naming words can be used instead of a particular naming word. Some substitute naming words are very *specific*. For example: *he* substitutes for *Imad* and *this* substitutes for *newspaper*. Other substitute naming words are more *general*. The words on this list are *general* words that can substitute for particular naming words:

other	another	some
anybody	anyone	anything
everybody	everyone	everything
nobody	no one	nothing
somebody	someone	something
both	none	several

We can use these *general* words when we do not want or need to name a *particular* person or thing.

Examples: I heard *Maria* complain. (particular)
I heard *someone* complain. (general)
Tom, Jorge, and Maria asked for a raise. (particular)
Some asked for a raise. (general)
The employees did not object to performance-based pay. (particular)
No one objected to performance-based pay. (general)

Some of these words refer to only one person, place, or thing. Others refer to more than one. Some can refer to *either* one or more than one.

- ***One person, place, or thing:*** another, anybody, anything, everybody, everyone, everything, nobody, no one, nothing, somebody, someone, something.

  Examples: Does *anybody* know if Sally went on vacation?
  Everything was discussed at the meeting.

- ***More than one person, place, or thing:*** both, several, some.

  Examples: *Both* want dental insurance.
  Some started this year.

- ***Either one or more than one person, place, or thing:*** other, none.

  Examples: This bolt is all right, but the *other* is not.
  Some workers have just been hired. *Others* have been here more than a year.
  The workers are unhappy, but *none* has complained.
  There are many tasks to do, but *none* are difficult.

TO LEARN MORE ABOUT SUBSTITUTE NAMING WORDS, STUDY CHAPTER 17.

Exercise 11.3

In the space provided, write a general substitute word to replace the particular naming word in the following sentences. The first sentence has been done for you. (The answer key is on page 190.)

1. Manuel said that we will get a raise.
   <u>Someone</u> said that we will get a raise.
2. Maria and Rosita want a day-care program.
   ______________ want a day-care program.
3. Do the employees want more money?
   Does ______________ want more money?
4. The workers do not want shorter hours.
   ______________ wants shorter hours.
5. Ming wants better lighting.
   ______________ wants better lighting.
6. The employees all want more benefits.
   The employees all want ______________.
7. The boss will try to do what the workers want.
   The boss will try to do ______________.
8. The whole group wants more vacation time.
   ______________ wants more vacation time.
9. Did Jorge disagree with the new wage plan?
   Did ______________ disagree with the new wage plan?
10. The workers will not get the benefits they asked for.
    The workers will get ______________.

Practice

Make up sentences that you could use when you talk to your boss or your co-workers.

- Be sure that some of your sentences use the helping words *should* and *should not*.
- Also make up sentences using *that* to connect two sets of words. Remember to use the special action words: *say, agree, demand, believe, propose, wish, think, prove, hope, decide, suggest, confess, see, assume, recommend*.
- In some of your sentences, substitute a *general* word for a *particular* naming word.

CHAPTER TWELVE

Going to School/Disagreeing

Going to school is a big decision—but it is worth it. Education is an investment that is never wasted. In this country—just as in your native country—education is the first ingredient for career success. It also can add pleasure and satisfaction to other parts of your life. If you want to go to school, you must do three things:

- Decide which school to attend.
- Become a student at the school.
- Understand how to do well in school.

Decide which school to attend

To decide which kind of school to attend, you must look at three things:

- How much time you have to go to class.
- How much money you have to spend on tuition and books.
- Your purpose in going to school.

Time. Most people do not have very much time for going to school. They have to work at their jobs eight hours a day—or more. They may only be able to take one course each semester or quarter. Or they may only be able to go to classes at a certain time of day—at night, in the morning, or in the afternoon. But some people have the time to take many courses at one time. They may be in a hurry to finish their coursework so they can get a good job or even to get *more* education at another school. Most schools let their students take as few or as many courses as they want to take. But some trade schools want their students to take several courses at the same time. Ask yourself: How much time do I have?

Money. People must pay tuition or a fee to go to school. The cost is different at different schools. For example, a course at a community

USEFUL WORDS

Action words	Naming words	Describing words
to attend (school)	education	educational
to admit to be admitted (to school)	admission	academic
to register (for school, for a class), to sign up	course, coursework	trade, technical
to enroll (in a class)	registration	formal/informal
to study, to learn	class, classroom	complete/incomplete
to assign (work, material, a lesson)	text, textbook	excellent
to do (an assignment, homework)	workbook	good
to take (notes, a test)	assignment	average
to pass	lesson	below average
to fail	homework	advanced
to finish, to complete	exercise, practice	remedial
to graduate	student	
to grade, to score	teacher, instructor	
to lecture	faculty	
	record, transcript	
	a graduate, graduation	
	grade, score	
	a lecture	
	tuition, fee	
	handout(s)	
	test, exam, examination	
	syllabus	
	diploma, degree, certificate	
	subject	
	semester, quarter	
	tutor	
	library	
	catalogue	
	lab, resource center, assistance center	
	counselor, adviser	

school may cost several dollars. But a course at a community/junior college will cost several *hundred* dollars. It would probably cost you several *thousand* dollars to earn a diploma or certificate at a trade school or college. But most schools want to help their students get the money for tuition and fees. They help people find out about different ways to get money for school—student loans, grants, and scholarships. Ask yourself: How much money do I have to pay for school? Even if you don't have much money, don't give up. You might be able to get some financial help from a school.

Purpose. People go to school for four different reasons:

1. They want to learn skills that will help them in life, such as speaking, reading, writing, and mathematics. If you are like these people, then you should think about going to high school,

KINDS OF SCHOOLS

Most cities have many different kinds of schools for adults. Here are some of the choices you have:

High school. In most cities and large towns, people can go to high school classes at night. These courses are for people who did not finish high school when they were young. The courses help these people prepare for a test called the General Educational Development test (GED). When they pass the GED, they get a high school diploma. Not everyone in these courses wants to take the GED test. Some people just want to learn more about a subject—like math or reading. To find out about these courses, look in the telephone book for the main office number for the public schools in your city. Someone in that office can tell you how to get into high school classes at night.

Language school. Many cities have schools to help people from other countries learn English. They teach their students how to speak, read, and write in English. Their students come from all over the world. To find out about these schools, look under "Language Schools" in the yellow pages of your telephone book.

Trade school. All cities have schools that teach people how to do a certain kind of work. Here are some of the different skills that trade schools teach: secretarial, computer, drafting, medical and dental assisting, welding, car repair, air conditioner and heater repair, electronics, security guard, accounting, bartending, hair cutting, and truck driving. In these schools, it takes from four or five months to as long as two or three years to complete all the courses in the program. To find out about these schools, look under these headings in your telephone book yellow pages: "Schools—Business & Secretarial," "Schools—Industrial & Technical & Trade," and "Schools—Medical & Dental Assistants & Technicians."

Community school. In many cities, classes are offered to people who want to learn without tests or grades. Community schools offer many different courses at many different times—and the fees are low. A course may only meet for one class, or it may meet for as many as twelve classes. Community schools are informal. That means the courses do not count in your formal education. To learn about the community school in your city, call the public library. Someone there will be able to give you information.

College. Your city may have a two-year college (called a community college or a junior college) or a four-year college. It also might have a university. Often, the courses at a community/junior college are not as hard for students as the courses at a college or university. Also, it usually is easier to be admitted to a community/junior college. These different kinds of colleges teach academic subjects—like science and history. Community/junior colleges also teach some of the same subjects that trade schools teach. Usually, you must have a high school diploma to go to a college. But some colleges let people without diplomas take courses as "special students."

community/junior college, or perhaps language school.

2. They want to learn skills that will help them get a better job. Some examples of these skills are typing, repairing cars, driving trucks, and cutting hair. If you are like these people, then you should think about going to trade school or community/junior college.

3. They want to learn more about our world. Maybe they want to learn about politics. Maybe they are interested in poems and stories. Maybe they want to learn about the laws of nature or about the way people think and feel. Some of these people want to study business or computers so they can get a good job. If you are like any of these people, then you should think about going to community/junior college. You could also go to a four-year college or a university.

4. They want to learn about things that will make their lives more fun, interesting, or healthy. For example, they might want to learn about dancing, art, cooking, or sewing. They might want to learn how to play a guitar or how to protect themselves from robbers. If you are like any of these people, you should think about going to a community school.

Ask yourself: Why do I want to go to school? What subjects do I want to learn about? How do I want to use my education?

When you have answered all of these questions about *time, money* and *purpose*, you are ready to look for a school. Ask people you know for information about schools in your city. Look in the yellow pages of your telephone book to find the names and phone numbers of some schools. Call for information. Most schools have a booklet or catalogue that gives all the information you need. Ask the school to mail you all their information, including an application form.

When you get information from all the schools, you can compare them. You can see how well each one fits with your time, money, and purpose in going to school. Also, you can see what each one expects from its students. Colleges and some trade schools expect you to have a high school diploma or GED. Some colleges also expect you to pass a special test before they will take you as a student. By comparing, you will be able to find the best school for you.

Become a student at the school

You must follow two steps to become a student:

- Apply for admission.
- Register for courses.

Apply for admission. The first step is to let the school know you are interested in becoming a student. You must apply for admission. The different kinds of schools have different rules for admitting students.

If you want to take courses at a *community school* or at a *night high school*, admission and registration are the same thing. You just write your name, address, phone number, and the courses you want to take on a form. Then you turn in the form along with the money to pay for your course fees. And that takes care of it.

If you want to take courses at a *community/junior college*, a *four-year college*, or a *university*, admission takes several steps:

1. Fill out an application form that asks for this information:
   - Name, address, and phone number.
   - Date and place of birth.
   - Social security or social insurance number.
   - Names of schools you went to, the years you were there, what you studies, the grades you made, and if you graduated.
   - Whether you were in the military service (Army, Navy, Marines, Air Force, Coast Guard, National Guard or Militia), the years you were there, and your rank.
   - The subjects you are interested in.

   Sometimes you also must write a paragraph or two about why you want to go to school. This is a way for the school to learn about you and your goals.

2. Arrange for your other school records to be sent to the school. This is a way for the school to learn what you have studied and the grades you have made. Most community/junior colleges, four-year colleges, and universities expect you to have a high school diploma or GED certificate. But some will admit you without them as a "special student."

3. Take a test. Most community/junior colleges, four-year colleges, and universities expect you to take a test before they will admit you as a student. The test will show the school what you already know. Some schools will admit you as a "special student" without a test.

Because they are companies, *language schools* and *trade schools* are different from some of the other schools. They are in business to make money from teaching. As with the other kinds of schools, you must fill out forms with certain basic information about yourself. At a language school, you also may take a test to find out which courses are right for you. But the language school probably won't care about your past education. On the other hand, most trade schools will expect you to have finished high school. If you don't have a high school diploma, some trade schools even have courses to help you pass the GED test. Then they will allow you to take the trade courses.

Register for courses. When you have been admitted to a school, you must sign up for the courses you want to take and pay the fees. You might take only one course, or you might take five or six courses. That depends upon the time and money you have for school. It also depends upon the courses the school offers and the rules about who is allowed to take certain courses. Most schools have counselors or advisers who can help you figure out what courses to take.

At a community school, you can take almost any course that is offered. At a language school, the school will tell you which courses are right for you—and usually you can take as many of those courses as you want. The same is usually true at high schools and trade schools. But at some trade schools, you are expected to take a certain group of courses at the same time.

At community/junior colleges, four-year colleges, and universities, you can register for many different kinds of courses. The school may offer 20 or 30 different subjects—and 10 or 20 courses about each subject. Certain courses are open to anyone who wants to attend. But others are only for students who are advanced in that subject. It is a good idea to talk to a counselor about the courses you want to take before you try to register.

Understand how to do well in school

To be a good student, you must follow two sets of rules:

- Rules for the classroom.
- Rules for outside the classroom.

Rules for the classroom. Get involved in your classes. If you want to learn as much as you can, here are some steps you should follow in your classes:

- *Attend the classes.* You cannot learn if you are not in class! Also, some teachers will make you leave the course or give you an F if you miss too many classes.

- *Follow your teacher's instructions.* On the first day of class, your teacher will tell you what textbooks and supplies you must have for the course. He or she will tell you when important things will happen—like a big test. Also, he or she will tell you what you must do to get a good grade in the class.

- *Take notes.* Take a notebook and a pen or pencil to your class. As your teacher lectures to the class, write down the most important things he or she says. Writing helps you understand the information. Also, the notes will help you study for tests.

- *Ask questions.* Sometimes you may not understand an idea that your teacher is talking about. It is important for you to *ask* your teacher to *explain* or to give an *example* of the idea. Ask your questions in class, so that other students can learn, too.

- *Speak during class discussions.* In some classes, the students spend time discussion the ideas and information that the teacher has presented. When you are in such a class, share your point of view with the other students. Don't sit quietly while others do all the speaking. You will learn better if you get involved. And the others may learn something from *you.*

Rules for outside the classroom. Sometimes, what you do when you are *not* in class is more important than what you do when you *are* in class. Here are some steps you should follow between class meetings:

- *Do assignments on time.* When your teacher tells the class to finish an assignment by a certain day, you must try to meet his or her schedule. Many teachers will give you a lower grade if your assignment is late.

- *Study regularly.* There are three kinds of studying: (1) reading (and reading again) in the textbook, (2) reading your notes from class, and (3) practicing what you have learned. For example, in a math class you need to practice solving math problems. (In some kinds of classes, there is nothing to practice. For example, in a history class, there are no skills to practice as in math.) Some students only study just before taking a test. That's a mistake! Study every week. You will understand the information better and you will make better grades.

• *Get help with your schoolwork.* Most schools have places you can go for tutoring. Sometimes they are called "resource centers" or "labs." These centers have just one job—to help students with their schoolwork. If you feel you could do better in your classes, then use the help that the school has provided for you. Also, go to your teacher for help. He or she will be glad to talk with you about the course.

REGISTERING FOR CLASSES: A SAMPLE CONVERSATION

Audelia Montoya is starting classes at Abbott Community College. She is meeting with her school counselor, Jan Browning, to figure out which classes she should take this semester.

Jan: Audelia, I see here in your file that you are aiming at a two-year degree in nursing.

Audelia: Yes, I want to be a Licensed Vocational Nurse. Right now I am working as a nurse's aide in Memorial Hospital. I think I could be a good nurse, and I'd like to earn more money than I do as an aide.

Jan: I think you've got a good plan. Since you work with nurses already, you know what they do. And you can learn from watching them and asking questions. Well, let's look at the course schedule and figure out what courses you should take this semester.

Audelia: I wrote down some classes I am interested in on this piece of paper. I work the evening shift, so I can take classes all day long.

Jan: Let me see what you have written down. Oh, Audelia! I think you might be asking too much of yourself. Six classes is a lot to take, even for students who aren't working at full-time jobs.

Audelia: But I want to finish all my coursework as quickly as possible. There are so many courses to take before I can get my degree. It could take forever!

Jan: I understand your eagerness, Audelia. But think about this: If you take six classes, you will be in class about four hours a day.

Audelia: But I have plenty of time before I go to the hospital at three o'clock. I have *seven* hours between eight in the morning and three in the afternoon.

Jan: I agree, you have a long period of time for classes during the day. But not all of your classwork is done *in class*, you know. You will have homework for every class you take. You will have library work to do and tests to study for.

Audelia: Well, I know that. But how long can that take? I'll have some extra time on my days off, too.

Jan: Here is a simple rule for figuring out how much time you must spend to be a good student: *For every hour you spend meeting in class, you must spend three hours preparing between classes.* Of course, this rule is only true *in general*. For some classes you spend less time and for others you spend more. And at some times during the semester, you spend more time on *every* class—like during exam week.

Audelia: Three hours for every class meeting... *every week?* That's a lot of hours! If I spend four hours in class every day, then that adds up to *twelve hours a day* outside class!

Jan: That's how much time you would have to spend to make good grades. Of course, if you don't care about making good grades, you could do a little less.

Audelia: But I want to be a good student...I want to be a good *nurse!*

Jan: You could take six courses and work *really* hard, but you also need time to sleep and eat and have some fun every now and then!

Audelia: I see your point. I guess I was biting off more than I can chew. So how many courses do you think I should take?

Jan: Well, I think you should start off with three this semester. If you can handle those, then maybe next semester you can take four courses.

Audelia: Okay. Let's decide on which ones I should register for tomorrow.

Jan: Okay!

DISCUSSING IDEAS: A SAMPLE CONVERSATION

One of the classes Audelia registered for is psychology—the study of how people think, feel, and act. Abbott Community College expects all nursing students to take a course in psychology. Audelia and her classmate Carolyn are talking after class about ideas they heard today from their teacher, Mr. O'Connor.

Audelia: I never realized how much people "say" without saying a word!

Carolyn: Me neither! I was amazed when Mr. O'Connor told us that people communicate with each other mostly with their faces and bodies.

Audelia: And the sound of their voices, not just the words they say!

Carolyn: It's interesting, but I'm not sure I really understand. When I look at it one way, what Mr. O'Connor said makes good sense. But when I look at it another way, I'm not so sure. Why do we spend so much time trying to say just the right words if they don't really count?

Audelia: Mr. O'Connor didn't say that words don't count at all. He just said that other things count more than we usually realize. Listen, I thought of an example. When someone is mad, how do we know?

Carolyn: Well, they say angry things. They tell us that something is bugging them. They are rude. They shout.

Audelia: Right, they *shout*. And they don't just shout about what's bugging them. They may shout about other things, too.

Carolyn: But when my boyfriend gets mad, he stops talking to me. Gives me the cold shoulder. What about that?

Audelia: That's an example, too. After all, its what he *does* that tells you he's angry, not what he *says*.

Carolyn: I'm still not sure I agree. What about people shouting when they *aren't* angry? Sometimes my boyfriend yells nice things when he is talking to me. He shouts things like "You're beautiful!" right in front of everyone. I know he's not angry! I believe his *words*, not his *voice*.

Audelia: I bet you believe more than just his *words*, Carolyn. Is he smiling? Does he have his arm around you? Those are ways of "saying" what he means, too.

Carolyn: Well, yes. I see what you mean. If he was frowning and standing with his hands on his hips, I probably would think he was insulting me instead of being nice.

Audelia: And what if he whispered "You're so ugly" very romantically in your ear while holding you close? Would you think he was insulting you or just teasing you?

Carolyn: You're right. I give up!

Audelia: Well, I've got to go to the library before it gets too late. I'll see you in class on Friday, okay?

Carolyn: Sure. See you then. Bye!

LANGUAGE SKILLS

People learn best when they get involved with the information they are studying. Getting involved in this way means asking questions and sometimes even debating over what something means. ***Disagreeing*** is an important part of learning. To disagree, you must be able to talk about the past and the future together. You also must be able to show how ideas are connected to each other. Here are two important language skills that you will need in order to ***disagree***:

- How to use action words to show connections between events in the past and the future.
- How to use connecting words to show relationships between ideas—*contrast, cause and effect*, and *possibility*.

Using Action Words

Certain action words can be used with helping words to show connections between:

- Two events in the past.
- Two events in the future.

Show the connection between *two events in the past* in these three ways:

- Use the words **was** or **were** + action word + **-ing** to talk about actions that continued to happen when another action occurred.

Use **was** when talking about yourself **(I)** or another person or thing **(he, she, it)**.
Use **were** when talking *about* more than one person or thing **(we, they)** or *to* another person or thing **(you)**.

Examples: They *were discussing* the problem when the professor arrived.
Inez *was arguing* with Gilbert about the answer when they got their tests back.

- Use the words **had** + **been** + action word + **-ing** to talk about actions that were happening which *stopped* when some other action occurred.

Use the same action word whether you are talking about *only one* person or thing or *more than one* person or thing.

Examples: The students in class *had been studying* bones until Dr. Javier gave his lecture on muscles.
I *had been reading* two or three magazines a week before I started going to school.

- Use the word **had** + action word + **-ed** to talk about actions that had already happened before another action happened.

Use the same action word whether you are talking about *only one* person or thing or *more than one* person or thing.

Examples: Everyone *had agreed* on a study schedule before Mrs. Yaffe announced a new assignment.
Shrinath *had finished* his essay before Susan told him about the change of topic.

Show the connection between *two events in the future* in these two ways:

- Use the words **will** + **have** + action word + **-ed** to talk about actions that will happen before or by the time another future action happens.

Use the same action word whether you are talking about *only one* person or thing or *more than one* person or thing.

Examples: We *will have answered* all the study questions by the time you get there.
Dilhan *will have delivered* his report before the class ends.

- Use the words **will** + **have** + **been** + action word + **-ing** to talk about actions that will be happening when another event occurs or when a certain time comes.

Use the same action word whether you are talking about *only one* person or thing or *more than one* person or thing.

Examples: I *will have been going* to school four years at the end of this semester.
Professor Horowitz *will have been lecturing* for half an hour by the time Carlos can get to class.

TO LEARN MORE ABOUT ACTION WORDS, STUDY CHAPTER 18.

Exercise 12.1

Here are some sentences about going to school. In the space beside each sentence, write the letters that describe the way the sentence connects two actions in the past or two actions in the future. The first sentence has been done for you. (The answer key is on page 190.)

PC: Something that *continued* to happen after another action in the past.

PSW: Something that stopped happening *when* another action in the past occurred.

PSB: Something that happened *before* another action in the past.

FB: Something that will happen *before* or *by the time* some other action happens in the future.

FW: Something that will be happening in the future *when* another event occurs.

PSW 1. Audelia had been hoping to take six classes before she talked to her school counselor, Jan Browning.

____ 2. Audelia will have taken only three classes by next spring.

____ 3. She had decided to study nursing even before working as a nurse's aide.

____ 4. Audelia was working the evening shift while she took classes during the daytime.

____ 5. Jan will have been counseling at Abbott Community College for six years this fall.

____ 6. She had been talking to students all morning before Audelia came in.

____ 7. Audelia will have been attending Abbott Community College for four years when she graduates.

____ 8. She had not expected to spend so many hours preparing between classes before she met with Jan.

____ 9. She will have developed a lot of discipline by the time she becomes a nurse.

Exercise 12.2

In this conversation, underline the action words that best tell the speaker's meaning. The first one has been done for you. (The answer key is on page 190.)

Bonnie: Aziz, you (1) **[were attending] [will have attended]** the community college last year. Why did you decide to attend trade school this year?

Aziz: I (2) **[had studied] [had been studying]** business for a year when I realized I didn't really like business!

Bonnie: So now you want to study electronics instead?

Aziz: Yes. I (3) **[was taking] [had been taking]** a computer course last semester that I found to be quite interesting. One day I realized that I (4) **[had been wondering] [will have been wondering]** all the time about how the computers worked. I was more interested in the computers than in the computer programs.

Bonnie: How do you like the new school so far? I (5) **[had heard] [was hearing]** that you could not get all the classes you want to take this semester.

Aziz: Actually, I (6) **[was just thinking] [had just been thinking]** about how much I enjoy this school when I came to meet you. Even though I can't take all the classes I want right now, I (7) **[will have been completing] [will have completed]** all the courses I need by the time I must go back to my country.

Bonnie: What will you do when you go back?

Aziz: Well, by then I (8) **[was studying] [will have been studying]** abroad for three years, so I think I will spend some time visiting with my family and friends. But after a few months, I think I (9) **[had been resting] [will have rested]** long enough. Then I will look for a job.

Bonnie: I guess you will deserve a rest by then! I wish you good luck.

Using Connecting Words

Certain connecting words connect two parts of a sentence together and at the same time show how those two parts are related to each other. These connecting words can show *contrast, cause and effect,* and *possibility*.

• When you want to show that two things are not related, you use connecting words that show *contrast:* **although, even though, even if.**

Examples: I want to be a secretary *although* I cannot type.
Joe is determined to finish school *even though* he has no money to pay for it.
The school will accept anyone as a student, *even if* he never got a high school diploma.

• When you want to show that one thing does affect another thing, you use connecting words that show *cause and effect:* **because, since.**

Examples: Imad made an A in the course *because* he studied hard.
They cannot taking Accounting II *since* they have not taken Accounting I.

• When you want to show how one thing *might* affect another thing, you use connecting words that show *possibility*: **if, unless.**

Examples: *If* I do well on this assignment, the teacher may let me skip the final exam.
Chih-Chao will make a C in English class *unless* he studies harder.

TO LEARN MORE ABOUT CONNECTING WORDS, STUDY CHAPTER 20.

Exercise 12.3

Complete the following sentences with a connecting word that shows *contrast, cause and effect,* or *possibility.* Before you write your answer, think carefully about which kind of relationship the parts of the sentence should have with each other. The first sentence has been done for you. (The answer key is on page 190.)

1. __Because__ Vicente does not have a high school diploma, he must take the GED test.
2. I want to study American history______________ it will not help me get a better job.
3. The teacher will not let me turn in my homework late ______________ I have a good excuse.
4. Barbara is studying to be a dental assistant ______________ her father is a dentist.
5. Malek will have to take another semester of English class ______________ he can pass the advanced placement exam.
6. ______________ Liu can take only one class this semester, she will be able to take four next semester.
7. We all received a B on the project ______________ the professor believed we should have worked harder.
8. ______________ the class on engine repair is full, Ramona will take the class on plumbing.
9. Eldon will not take cooking lessons ______________ he has to eat sandwiches for the rest of his life.
10. My English has improved quite a bit ______________ I practice talking with my friend Jane.

Practice

Make up sentences about your experiences in school in the past or your plans for school in the future. Use helping and action words to show how two events are connected in the past or the future. Also use connecting words—*although, even though, even if, because, since, if,* and *unless*—to show contrast, cause and effect, or possibility.

CHAPTER THIRTEEN

Buying a Car or Other Major Item/Advising

When people make a major purchase—like a car, a clothes washer and dryer, or living-room furniture—they usually feel excited. But because they are spending a lot of money, they want to be sure they are making a good decision. Here are some steps to follow when you want to buy a car or other major item:

- Compare brands, models, and prices.
- Look at different financing choices.
- Choose the deal that best fits your needs and your budget.

Compare brands, models, and prices

Before you make a major purchase such as furniture or appliances, ask yourself several questions. We will talk about cars, but you should ask the same questions about any major purchase.

- *Should I buy something new or used?* You can buy a used car at a lower cost, but you could have more repair costs than on a new item. If you can fix the problem yourself, you could save money. If you decide to look for a used car, decide how old it can be and whether you will buy it from a dealer or from an individual.
- *What size should I buy?* Cars come in different sizes. The smallest cars are called minis. Then come subcompacts, compacts, midsized sedans, sedans, station wagons, vans, and utility vehicles. In general, the smaller the car, the lower the price—but not always. Sports cars are small and can be very expensive. Price also depends on special features and on the brand. Economy cars are those that cost a small amount for their size and do not have fancy features. Luxury cars have many special features no matter what size they are.

USEFUL WORDS

Action words	Naming words	Describing words
to shop for	vehicle	new
to visit (a showroom)	car	used
to drive	truck	2-door
to test-drive	sports car	4-door
to borrow (money)	station wagon	luxury
to finance (a car or big purchase)	utility vehicle	economy
	van/wagon	hatchback
to negotiate	compact	American
to buy	sedan	foreign
to invest in	model, brand	convertible
to sign (a contract)	body	utility
to compare (prices)	dealership	2-wheel drive
to make a deal	new-car dealer	4-wheel drive
	used-car dealer	sport
	sticker price	compact
	purchase price	two-seater
	trade-in	
	down payment	
	rebate	
	warranty	
	extended service	
	TTL (taxes, title, and license)	
	insurance	
	inspection	
	fuel economy	
	loan	
	monthly payment	
	interest rate	
	sales contract	
	price range	
	consumer loan	
	inspection sticker	
	used-car lot	

• *What features do I need?* If you have several people in your family, you may want a car with four doors so those in the back can get in and out easily. Do you want a standard transmission that requires you to shift by hand or do you want an automatic transmission? You will need to decide on special features such as a larger engine for more power, air conditioning, a tape deck, or a sunroof.

• *How much can I pay?* There are two ways to pay. You might pay in cash all at one time. If you do, you can usually get a lower price on large items. Some people believe in saving their money until they can do this. But most people finance expensive purchases. To finance a purchase means to pay part of the total price—called a down payment—and then pay the remainder in monthly payments. When you buy a car, your old car can sometimes be the down payment—or part of the down payment. If you choose to finance, decide how much money you have for a down payment and how much you can pay each month.

Once you have answered these questions, do some research to find more information. Here are several ways to research:

• *Read* Consumer Reports *magazine.* You can find *Consumer Reports* in any library. Ask the librarian to help you find the latest report on the item you want to buy. *Consumer Reports* does its own testing and research. You can find out what brands and models have the best rating and what problems came up during the tests. You can also find out the cost.

• *Ask your friends and co-workers for advice.* See if you can find someone who has owned a car like the one you want to buy. Ask about the kinds of problems people have had with their cars. Note which car models and brands seem to need the most repairs. Ask an auto mechanic what he thinks.

• *Read newspaper advertisements for used items, even if you're looking for something new.* Note the number of ads for different brands and models of used cars. If there are many ads for a particular make of car, find out if that model or brand has some problem that causes the previous owners to sell. Note the price and compare it with the purchase price. Has the car kept its value or did it drop? The value of a used car is listed in a special book, called the Blue Book. Sometimes you can buy a Blue Book in a bookstore for a few dollars. Cars sometimes cost more than the Blue Book price. For example, a car with very few miles on it may cost more. But a car that has been in an accident or is in bad shape may cost less than the Blue Book price.

When you have done some research and know what features you want, how much you can afford to spend, how you will pay, and whether you want a new or used item, then look for yourself.

Go to several car dealerships, either new or used. You will find them listed in the yellow pages under "Automobile Dealers," or in newspaper advertisements. You may even want to look at some cars for sale by individuals. They may advertise their cars in the classified section of the newspaper or put a "For Sale" sign in the car window. One advantage of buying a new car from a dealership is the new-car warranty, which is the dealer's guarantee to take care of any problems with the car for a certain period of time. Dealerships often offer warranties on their used vehicles as well, though the used-car warranties are usually for a shorter time and cover fewer problems than new-car warranties.

Do not buy the first car you see. Be sure to look around first. Look for the sticker price, which is the price listed on a sticker attached to the car. Many things can change the sticker price, such as the amount of your down payment, the way you pay for the car, the special features you want, and extra warranties and services you may buy. You will want to make a deal with the person selling the car to get the most for your money.

Often, when buying from an individual you can make a deal to pay less than the asking price. Remember that when you buy from an individual, you are not likely to get a warranty with the car, so you must pay for any repairs the car may need. When buying from an individual, remember to:

1. Compare several cars to make the best deal.
2. Try to get the owner to lower his asking price.
3. Have the car checked by a mechanic before you buy.
4. Be sure to get the car's title in the deal.

Look at different financing choices

How do you pay for a major purchase? First, you must plan. Think about how much money you have available now and how much you could pay each month.

Some people save their money until they can buy it with cash all at one time. If you decide to buy with cash, the seller will often lower the price of the item you are buying.

TIPS ON BUYING FURNITURE AND APPLIANCES

Buying furniture. You can buy furniture at several places. Most department stores have furniture departments. Some stores sell only one type of furniture, such as kitchen tables and chairs. Some stores sell one furniture style, such as modern or country. You can find some furniture, such as outdoor furniture, as supermarkets.

Some stores sell furniture that costs a lot and some stores sell "budget" furniture. Discount stores often carry furniture at a low price. Furniture stores often compete for your business, so you may see advertisements for stores that are "going out of business" or for "last sale of the season." Some stores have had "going out of business" sales for years!

Look in the yellow pages of the telephone book under "Furniture Dealers—Retail." You'll find the names and addresses of furniture dealers near you. If you want to know if the store sells high-priced furniture or budget furniture, call and ask what the price range is on the item you want to buy. The price range means a guess about the lowest price and the highest price sold in the store.

You can buy used furniture through classified advertisements in the newspaper. Look under "Merchandise—Furniture." Call the telephone number listed and ask about the item you want to buy. If it sounds like something you want, ask to see it. After you have looked at it, you can decide if you want to buy it or not. You can also get used furniture at garage sales, flea markets, and secondhand stores.

Buying appliances. Appliances are sold at department stores and appliance stores. Like cars, most new appliances come with warranties that cover service and parts if something goes wrong. You can buy high-priced appliances or budget appliances. Look in the yellow pages under "Appliances—Household." You can find out if a store sells budget or higher-priced appliances by calling to ask the price range on their appliances. Then visit the store to see them.

You can also lease appliances. A lease is a way to rent an appliance for a period of time. With some leases you can choose to buy the appliance later. When you lease, you do not have to make a down payment, but you must make monthly payments. You may have to make a deposit, but the deposit is usually smaller than a down payment would be. If you take care of your appliance, you can get your deposit back when you return the appliance.

Buying electronic equipment. Electronic equipment—such as sound systems, tape decks, radios, and television sets—can be bought at special electronics stores, at department stores, and often at supermarkets. Some stores sell only the best, and most expensive, electronics. Others sell electronic products for people on a budget. Look for electronics stores in the yellow pages of the telephone book under the item you want to buy, such as "Radios—Dealers," "Stereophonic & High Fidelity Equipment—Dealers," or "Television—Dealers." Call and ask for a price range on the item you want to buy. Then you can shop at the store later.

Often the stores that carry expensive electronic equipment also have some used equipment for sale. You can also buy used electronic equipment at garage sales, in flea markets, and through the classified advertisement section of the newspaper. Look under "Merchandise." Before you buy, be sure to check used equipment to see if it is still working. You probably won't get a warranty with used electronic equipment.

Most people decide to buy major items on credit, which means they decide to finance their purchase. Financing means you make a down payment of about 10–20 percent of the cost and you pay the rest in smaller monthly payments.

When you finance something, you also pay an interest charge. Interest charges can add a lot of cost to your purchase. Be sure to ask how much you will be paying in interest charges. The total amount of interest will vary, depending on how long you will be making payments.

How you pay for your major purchase often depends on where you buy it. Dealerships, department stores, and stores with expensive merchandise will often finance your purchase for you. To buy, you fill out a credit application at the store where you've made your choice. The person who sells you the item will guide you

MAKING A LOAN APPLICATION AT A BANK, CREDIT UNION, OR CREDIT COMPANY

A bank, credit union, or credit company will lend you money if they think you will repay them. You can find the names and addresses in the yellow pages of the telephone book. Before you apply for such a loan, call several places to find out their interest rate. You want to find the lowest interest rate, so the cost of your loan will be as low as possible.

When you're ready to discuss making a loan, go to the bank, credit union, or credit company and ask for the consumer loan department. Someone will help you. Ask that person to explain all the details of the loan, including the interest rate and the amount of money you will be paying in total interest. Find out how much they charge for late payments. See if you qualify for a loan at that institution. If not, go to another.

through the paperwork. The advantage is that it's easy. The disadvantage is that the financing, like the item, can be expensive.

If you have good credit, you can usually get a loan from your bank, a credit union, or a credit company. "Good credit" means that you have paid everyone you agreed to pay, including department stores, gas companies, and your rent. In addition to good credit, you have to show that you can afford to pay for the item with your present income. Before anyone will lend you money, they will ask for your financial history. They will check the information you give with the information about you at the local credit bureaus. Credit bureaus collect financial information about people. When you apply for a loan, the credit bureau will tell if you are behind in payments to other companies, if you have been late making payments, and how many times you have been late.

The advantage of getting a loan from a bank, a credit union, or a credit company is that you can shop around to get the lowest interest rate. That could lower the total cost to you. But shopping for a lower interest rate takes more time than getting financing from the company where you are making your purchase.

Choose the deal that best fits your needs and your budget

The process of shopping for a major item can get confusing. There are so many choices and prices it's hard to figure out what is best for you. Use this plan to help you decide:

1. Make several columns down a piece of paper. At the top of each column, write something you think is important about the item you are planning to buy. For example, if you are buying a car, you might have a column for automatic or standard transmission, a column for sunroof, a column for warranty, and a column for service. Leave the last column for price.
2. On lines across the page, list the different items you have seen and where you saw them. For example, if you're buying a car, you might list a Nissan at Stan's Motors. Across from it, make notes about the car you saw. In the transmission column, write "standard" if the car you looked at had standard transmission. You could also write in the different costs of the car with standard or automatic transmission, if both are available. In this way, write notes about all the cars you are interested in.
3. Consider the cars on your page. If none seems perfect, keep looking for the deal that fits both your needs and your bank account.

ADVISING A FRIEND: A SAMPLE CONVERSATION

Hung Wu is looking for a new car. Over lunch, he is talking with his boss, Zu-Yi Lee, about cars.

Hung: What kind of car should I buy, Zu-Yi? I need something for the family. We have two children now, and one is still a baby. I'd like to get something we can use for long trips as well as taking the children around town.

Zu-Yi: Well, we have a van. It's a little big for town driving, but we like it when we travel. I feel the children are safe in such a large vehicle. They have lots of room to play games in the back.
Hung: We thought about a van, but I understand they are not very fuel-efficient.
Zu-Yi: It isn't as good as the compact we had before. But it's better than most of the vans on the market. *Consumer Reports* said it's the most fuel-efficient of any of the vans.
Hung: Did it compare vans with station wagons? We'd thought about a full-sized station wagon.
Zu-Yi: I don't remember the numbers exactly, but I do remember that the van was less efficient than station wagons. We decided against the station wagon because we got a better price on the van. The dealer was running a special sale, so we got our van much cheaper than what we could have bought a station wagon for.
Hung: Well, I like the style of the station wagon better than a van's. My wife says she doesn't care as long as there is room for all the equipment she needs to carry for the baby. Our subcompact just isn't big enough any more. We need a larger car.
Zu-Yi: My uncle works at a dealership north of town. He was telling me about a sale they're going to start next month. You might be able to get a station wagon cheaper if you wait until then. Here is his card.
Hung: Thanks. That sounds like a good idea. I'll go see what he has.

COMPARING TWO THINGS: A SAMPLE CONVERSATION

Hung Wu is shopping for a station wagon at a dealership. Hui Wan, the uncle of Zu-Yi, is helping him. They are discussing two used station wagons.
Hung: From the outside, this brown one looks better than the blue one. Why is the blue one more expensive?
Hui: The blue one has an automatic transmission and a larger engine. It also has less usage. The brown one just had a paint job because it was in a fender-bender accident. The entire right fender is new.
Hung: Did they have to work on the engine at all?
Hui: No. The fender was the worst problem. The hood was dented a little, but not even as much as these dents on the blue car.
Hung: What do you know about the owners of the cars?
Hui: Well, you won't find a better driver than the owner of this blue car. She drove it just once or twice a week. The inside is in better shape than the brown's. The seats are less worn and the dashboard is more attractive. The radio gets more stations and has better speakers.
Hung: What did you say about the usage on the two cars?
Hui: The blue car has been driven less than the brown car. The owner of the brown car was a salesman who used the car for business.

MAKING A CREDIT APPLICATION AT A STORE

1. Get a credit application form. Often, you'll find them in cardboard stands on the counters at the store. If not, go to the store's office and ask for one. You can fill it out at home or at the store. The application will ask for:

- Your name, address, and telephone number.
- The name of your bank and the number of any accounts, including your checking and savings accounts.
- The name and number of other credit accounts you may have. They'll ask how much you owe on each one.
- The amount you make each month and how much of it you must spend on housing, food, and other regular payments. If two people bring in income, both can be considered part of the household income.

2. Send or take the application to the store. Either in person or on the telephone, someone may ask you for more information. If your application is approved, in a few weeks you will have a credit card. If you are in the store to buy a large item, you can sometimes get credit on the spot.

Hung: Which car do you recommend?
Hui: I'd suggest the blue car. It's exterior looks worse than the brown car's, but it has less wear and tear, a better interior, automatic transmission, a better radio and speakers, and I know the previous owner. This car is in better shape than most cars the same age.
Hung: What about financing? What kind of terms can you give me? My bank will loan me the money at 9.5 percent. Can you do better than that?
Hui: No. In fact, we are making loans at 10.5 percent right now. We just can't compete with the better terms of a good bank.
Hung: Do you give warranties with your used cars?
Hui: Yes, we do. In fact, we have the best warranty in town. I'll guarantee parts and service on either of these cars for 90 days.
Hung: That sounds good. Well, thank you for your time. I want to discuss these cars with my wife. Then I'll bring her in to see them, if we're still interested.

LANGUAGE SKILLS

When you are buying a major item, you will probably feel more confident about your decision if you get advice from others. Likewise, your friends may ask *you* for advice before making an important purchase. *Advising* involves both sharing what you know with others and helping them see all sides of their decision.

In this chapter, you will learn two important language skills for giving advice:

- How to use describing words to compare two or more things.
- How to use connecting words to compare two things.

Using Describing Words

Some describing words compare one thing with another. Add **-er** when you compare two things. Add **-est** when you compare three or more things.

Examples: The blue radio is *big*.
The black radio is *bigger* than the blue radio.
The white radio is the *biggest* radio we have.
This car is *pretty*.
The blue one is *prettier*.
The brown one is *prettiest* of all.

Some describing words compare by adding words like **more** and **most, less** and **least, better** and **best, worse** and **worst**.

Examples: The furniture is *beautiful*.
The furniture over there is *more beautiful*.
The furniture at the other store is the *most beautiful*.

TO LEARN MORE ABOUT DESCRIBING WORDS, STUDY CHAPTER 19.

Exercise 13.1

Here are some sentences that have a describing word. Complete the sentences that follow by changing the describing word to show comparison between two or more than two things. The first sentence has been done for you. (The answer key is on page 190.)

1. The brown car looked __clean__.
   The blue car looked __cleaner__ than the brown car.
   The white car is the _______ of all.

2. The standard transmission is easy to drive.
   The automatic transmission is _______ to drive.

3. The brown car is in __good__ shape.
   The blue car is in _______ shape.
   The new car is in the _______ shape.
4. I had a __bad__ day.
   His day was _______ .
   But she had the _______ day of all.
5. This car is __not__ expensive,
   but the smaller car is _______ expensive
   and the mini car is the _______ expensive.

Using Connecting Words

When you're comparing two things, you will often need to use connecting words that show this kind of relationship. Here are pairs of connecting words that compare:

more . . . than
less . . . than
as . . . as
so . . . that

Here are some examples of these connecting words in action:
The red car has *more* features *than* the blue car.
The white car is *as* pretty *as* the red car.
The power is *so* great *that* you can easily enter the freeway.

TO LEARN MORE ABOUT CONNECTING WORDS, STUDY CHAPTER 20.

Exercise 13.2

Use comparative connecting words to complete the following sentences. (The answer key is on page 190.)

1. The blue furniture has _______ seating _______ the green furniture.
2. The color is _______ bright _______ it would be hard to look at.
3. The small car is _______ expensive _______ the van.
4. The big refrigerator is _______ energy-efficient _______ the small one.
5. The cost is _______ great _______ we would need to finance the purchase.
6. The advantages are _______ great _______ we can't say no.
7. The big washing machine can hold _______ laundry _______ the small one.

Practice

Make up sentences that offer advice to someone (perhaps even yourself) about making an important purchase. Be sure to use describing words to compare *two* things (by adding *-er* to the end of the describing word or *more* in front of the describing word) and to compare *more than two* things (by adding *-est* to the end of the describing word or *most* in front of the describing word.) Also use pairs of connecting words to compare two things: *more . . . than, less . . . than, as . . . as,* and *so . . . that*.

CHAPTER FOURTEEN

Going to a Social Event/Introducing

As you make new friends in this country, you will be invited to different kinds of social events—dinners, parties, weddings, and more. And, of course, you may want to invite your friends to social events, too. Here are some things that you should know about:

- Attending formal social events.
- Attending informal social events.
- Planning a social event of your own.

Attending formal social events

• *First, the invitation comes.* A printed invitation comes in the mail. The invitation will ask you to attend a special event, such as a wedding. It tells you the names of the people giving the wedding, the names of the people getting married, the time and date, and the location.

Formal dinner party invitations may give one time for cocktails and another time for dinner. Sometimes the ending time is given as well. The invitation may include the style of clothing you're expected to wear, such as "black-tie" or "formal."

• *You say if you will be going or not.* Most formal invitations include the letters RSVP followed by a telephone number. RSVP means you are asked to call to say whether you will be attending or not. Some invitations include an envelope and a card for you to send your RSVP by mail. It is extremely impolite to ignore an RSVP.

• *You choose something to wear.* If an invitation calls for formal attire, for men that means a tuxedo and for women it means an evening dress. But few events call for formal clothing anymore. For a wedding women wear nice dresses, heels, and hose. Men wear suits.

• *Buy a gift.* If you have been invited to a wedding, it is proper to call someone in the wedding party to ask where the couple have registered for china and silver. Registering

USEFUL WORDS

Action words	Naming words	Describing words
to invite	dinner	elegant
to receive an invitation	party	formal
to attend	wedding	informal
to arrive	christening	gracious
to leave	graduation	well-mannered
to wear	banquet	black-tie
to telephone	cocktails	beautifully
to write	RSVP	
to visit	receiving line	
to celebrate	brunch	
to take a gift	barbecue	
to dance	picnic	
to play	reception	
to talk	potluck supper	
to RSVP	wedding shower	
to decline	baby shower	
to change your plans	invitation	
to introduce	food	
	entertainment	
	host	
	hostess	
	social event	
	ceremony	

means the couple has told a store which china and silver they want. You can go to the store and buy some pieces of it as your wedding gift. You can also ask what else the couple needs, if you like. Wrap the gift in gift-wrapping paper. Take the gift with you to the wedding, but leave it in the car during the ceremony and bring it to the reception, where a table will be set aside for gifts.

If you've received an invitation to a christening, you may take a small gift to the ceremony or send a card of congratulations in the mail if you cannot attend. If you've received an invitation to a graduation, you might send a small gift or card in the mail; you do not usually bring it to the graduation ceremony. No gifts are necessary for banquets, balls, or dinners.

• *Arrive on time.* In fact, for a wedding or graduation you are expected to arrive a little early so you can be seated before the ceremony begins. For formal dinners, you arrive during the cocktail hour and remain through dinner.

• *Speak to all the people hosting the event.* If this is a wedding, you are expected to greet the couple getting married and the parents on both sides. Most weddings will include a receiving line, where the hosts and hostesses say hello to their guests. It is proper to go down the receiving line and greet everyone. In a proper receiving line, each person in the line introduces you to the next person in line. However, that system often doesn't work. You may find that you need to introduce yourself to someone in the line who is a stranger.

At large dinner parties, balls, or graduation ceremonies, you may have to make a greater effort to greet your host and hostess. But do so.

• *Leave at a reasonable hour*. If the invitation says an event is over at a certain hour, it is polite to leave at that hour. The hostess will thank you, even if everyone else lingers. For a wedding, you may leave anytime after the bride and groom have gone. However, wedding parties often continue for hours after the bride and groom leave.

Attending informal social events

In this country, most people's social lives are informal. You are more likely to get a telephone call or a handwritten note than a printed invitation.

• Evening parties centering on informal socializing, drinks, and snack food are still given, but they are losing their popularity. You may find more board games being played, such as chess. Because these parties often span several hours, you can come and go at any time.

• Dinner parties can be very informal, such as barbecues, or more formal, such as sit-down dinners at home with fancy china and silver. If you get an invitation to dinner, be sure to RSVP so the hosts can prepare enough food. Do not change your mind except for a crisis, such as an illness. For a formal sit-down dinner, usually a woman would wear a nice dress, heels, and hose; a man would wear a suit or a sport jacket.

• Potluck suppers are very informal dinner parties. You are asked to bring a dish of food that will be put on the table along with everyone else's dish. The food is shared. Church groups and sports groups often hold potluck suppers. Dress is usually very casual, including jeans and shorts in warm weather.

• A picnic is sitting on a blanket outside eating food taken in a basket. Picnics are very casual and sports clothes appropriate to the season can be expected.

• Birthday parties are very popular in this country, especially for children but also for grown-ups. Surprise birthday parties are often given for people turning 30, 40, and 50. Be sure to take a gift to the birthday person.

• Seasonal parties include celebrations for Halloween, Christmas and Hanukkah, New Year's Eve, etc. These celebrations are often family-centered but include friends of the family as well.

On Halloween, people dress in costumes. The children often go house to house saying "Trick or treat!" At every door they are given candy or treats. Costumed Halloween parties for grown-ups are becoming more popular.

The Christmas season spans the month of December. A Christmas tree is decorated in many homes and under it people put presents for each other. There are many Christmas parties and special events, such as choirs performing seasonal music and ballet productions of *The Nutcracker*, a Christmas story.

The Jewish holiday Hanukkah also comes in December. It is celebrated for eight days by the lighting of a special candelabrum called a menorah. There are also many parties for family and friends.

New Year's Eve is a celebration to welcome the new year. It is held on December 31 with kisses and champagne flowing at exactly midnight when the new year comes in. Many parties are held and formal dress is sometimes needed.

Valentine's Day is a day for sweethearts. People give flowers or gifts to their spouses or boyfriends and girlfriends. Couples spend time together. Children exchange valentine cards at school. There are few group parties, but it is a time when couples go out for a special evening together.

The Fourth of July is Independence Day for the United States. It is the day for fireworks, speeches, and red-white-and-blue picnics or barbecues. Jeans, shorts, and swimsuits are usually worn.

• Special events are often reason enough for a party. Perhaps someone has gotten an honor or promotion at work or someone is retiring. Maybe a couple is finally going on a trip and their friends want to wish them bon voyage. All these celebrations can become parties, if people want to.

HOW TO DECLINE INFORMAL INVITATIONS

Sometimes you will be asked to attend informal events that you cannot or do not want to attend. It is perfectly proper to say, "I'm sorry. I won't be able to go." If you have to, you can make up an excuse, saying, "I've already made plans."

Sometimes you may need to change plans you've made to attend a party. Be sure to call the host or hostess and explain, saying, "I'm sorry. I had intended to come, but now I can't. I look forward to seeing you soon."

Planning a social event of your own

• *Decide what you want to do.* Will it be a party, a dinner, a picnic? Choose a date that gives you plenty of time to prepare.

• *Issue invitations.* If it is a casual, last-minute gathering of good friends, call people on the telephone and invite them. If you must give directions to your home, you may want to sent out written invitations that include a map, so you don't have to explain so many times.

If you're giving a sit-down dinner, written invitations with an RSVP are needed. You will want to know for sure how many people are coming so you can prepare the table and the food.

• *Decide what food you will have.* Try a pot-luck supper. Ask each person to bring a dish. You can even have them tell you if their dish will be a meat dish, a fruit dish, a vegetable dish, or a dessert. You provide the plates and silverware, the drinks, and one large main dish. Clear a table and set out the other dishes as they come. When everything is ready, let people walk around the table, filling their own plates. This is an easy party to have if you are on a budget.

You may prefer to give a large party and serve "finger food." If so, estimate the number of people who will be coming so you can plan how much food to buy and prepare. Cheese and crackers, chips with hot and cold dips, cut vegetables and fruit, small sausages, meatballs, and chicken wings are all popular party snack foods.

• *Party entertainment can be simple.* Many people like to listen to music, dance, and play board games, like chess and Scrabble. Some people may enjoy playing with a Frisbee in the yard. Think about using different rooms in your home for different activities.

• *Let your guests know when the party will begin and end.* Many people will arrive at a party late unless the invitation gives a beginning and ending time (like a cocktail party) or states that dinner will be served at a certain time (like a sit-down dinner party).

ACCEPTING AN INVITATION: A SAMPLE CONVERSATION

Ming Wang is calling her boss, Mrs. Wu, to RSVP for a baby shower. She dials the number.

Mrs. Wu: Hello.

Ming: Hello. Is this Mrs. Wu?

Mrs. Wu: Yes, it is.

Ming: Mrs. Wu, this is Ming Wang.

Mrs. Wu: Well, hello. I'm glad to hear from you. Can you come to the shower?

Ming: Yes. I'm looking forward to it.

Mrs. Wu: I am, too.

Ming: What does Lee need for the baby right now?

Mrs. Wu: Well, she's been saying she really needs some nightgowns for newborns. She says she likes the kind that have a drawstring at the bottom. Do you know what she means?

Ming: Yes, I do. I have a friend whose baby wears them.

Mrs. Wu: Ming, do you know how to get to my home?

Ming: No, I don't. I know you live near the Johnsons.

Mrs. Wu: Yes. I live right across the street. My address is 1401 Daybreak Hill. Do you know where that is?
Ming: Isn't it off Thirty-fourth Street near the bakery?
Mrs. Wu: Yes, that's right. Turn right off Thirty-fourth on Daybreak Hill. I'm the fourth house on the left.
Ming: Thanks. Is there anything I could bring to help you with the party?
Mrs. Wu: Not that I can think of, thank you.
Ming: I'll see you at the party, then?
Mrs. Wu: Yes. I'll see you at the party.

GETTING ACQUAINTED: A SAMPLE CONVERSATION

Lin-Lin and Huey Yang are talking to Ming Wang and her friend Tran Thai at a party. Lin-Lin and Ming work together.
Lin-Lin: Hi, Ming! I was hoping to see you here tonight!
Ming: Lin-Lin, I'm glad to see you, too. I don't know very many people here, I'm afraid. It's good to see a familiar face.
Lin-Lin: Ming, do you remember my husband, Huey. Huey, this is Ming Wang, my friend from work.
Ming: Of course I remember him! Hello, Huey. How have you been?
Huey: Very well, Ming. It's good to see you again.
Ming: You, too. Now, Lin-Lin, let me introduce you to my friend Tran Thai. Tran, this is Lin-Lin Yang and her husband, Huey.
Lin-Lin: Hello, Tran.
Huey: Hi, Tran. It's nice to meet you. You look very familiar to me. Maybe we have met before. Where do you work?
Tran: I have been driving a taxi for Cio Cabs for the past year. How about you? What do you do?
Huey: I work at the Hamburger Haven, down near the university.
Ming: Tran, Huey has a reputation as the best cook at Hamburger Haven. I love to go there just to eat his steak-k-bobs. They are delicious!
Lin-Lin: Ming, did you know that Huey invented that dish for the restaurant? Now it is one of their most popular dishes.
Ming: No, I didn't know that! I hope they gave you a big pay raise, Huey! You deserve it.
Huey: Thank you, Ming. It's nice to be appreciated. Well, Tran, how do you like it in this country? How long have you been here?
Tran: I came here by boat two years ago. How long have you been here?
Huey: Lin-Lin and I made the same trip by boat three years ago. did you come through the Philippines?
Tran: Yes. I had to stay in the refugee detention center for six months.
Lin-Lin: So did we. That was a scary time.
Huey: There have been many things to adjust to, but we have been so happy since we got to this country.
Lin-Lin: Tran, where are you living now?
Tran: I live just down the street from Ming. We met when we were running.
Ming: Yes. Tran has been telling me how much fun it is to compete in a running race.
Huey: Have you ever won a race, Tran?
Tran: No, not really. Not unless you count the race I won against my younger brother when we chased around the house as kids!
Lin-Lin: All this talk about running is making me hungry. I'm going to get some snacks over at the food table. Anybody want me to bring something back?
Huey: I'm hungry, too. I'll go with you.
Ming: Let's all go. Looks like Tran needs a refill on his drink.
Tran: You bet. This party is turning out to be a lot of fun!

LANGUAGE SKILLS

Social events bring people together—often people who have not met before. As a guest at a social event, you can make new friends by ***introducing*** yourself to people you don't know. As the host or hostess of a social event, you must ***introduce*** people to each other and help them get acquainted.

The following language skills will help you introduce yourself and others:

- How to use naming words to refer to yourself and others.
- How to use describing words to give more information.

Using Naming Words

Certain substitute naming words are used when the action reflects back on the person or thing who is doing it. These words are called *reflexive*. Here are the reflexive naming words:

myself	ourselves
yourself	yourselves
himself	themselves
herself	
itself	

Here are some examples of how these words are used:

Examples: I wake *myself* with my own snoring.
The dog scratched *itself* behind the ear.
He felt ashamed of *himself* for his mistake.

Here are some examples of the other reflexive naming words:

Examples: Try to control *yourselves*, boys!
You should see *yourself* in that silly mask.
Lupe heard *herself* saying "yes" when she meant "no."
We found *ourselves* in a hall of mirrors.
The winning team deserve to pat *themselves* on the back.

TO LEARN MORE ABOUT SUBSTITUTE NAMING WORDS, STUDY CHAPTER 17.

Exercise 14.1

Here are some sentences that can use reflexive naming words. Write the best reflexive naming word in the space provided. The first sentence has been done for you. (The answer key is on page 190.)

1. The baby wants to do it __herself__.
2. I ______________ think it's a good idea.
3. Tell ______________ that some good comes from all bad.
4. She wants to do it for ______________, not for the others.
5. My cat likes to wash ______________ after eating dinner.
6. Look, you can see ______________ in the television.
7. We only have ______________ to blame.
8. They can't see ______________ as others see them.
9. "Why me?" he kept asking ______________.
10. I threw ______________ on the bed and cried for hours.

Using Describing Words

Certain connecting words are also describing words. They connect a group of descriptive words to the rest of the sentence. This section will look at the word groups that describe a person, place, or thing. Here is a list of the special connecting/describing words: **who, whose,** and **which**.

Examples: The woman *who said hello* is my neighbor.
(*who said hello* describes "the woman")
The doctor, *whose family was with him*, stopped to help.
(*whose family was with him* describes "the doctor")

- To describe *people*, use the words **who** and **whose** to begin the describing word group.
  Example: The man *who invited me* is an old friend.
  (*who invited me* describes "the man")

- To describe *places*, use the word **which** to begin the describing word group.
  Example: The party will be at my cousin's house, *which is next door.*
  (*which is next door* describes "house")

- To describe *things*, use the word **which** to begin the describing word group.
  Example: Hope, *which never dies*, is all I have.
  (*which never dies* describes "hope")

TO LEARN MORE ABOUT DESCRIBING WORDS, STUDY CHAPTER 19.

Exercise 14.2

In the sentences below, underline all the words in the describing word group. Then circle the special describing word that begins each describing word group. The first sentence has been done for you. (The answer key is on page 190.)

1. We took care of some children whose mothers were working.
2. She introduced him to a woman who worked in her office.
3. Ming learned card games, which Tran liked to play.
4. Huey introduced Lin-Lin to the man who needed a secretary.
5. They stayed at the camp, which was in the Philippines.
6. No one whose mind is working right could possibly like that music.
7. Even ice cream, which she loved to eat, did not cheer her up.
8. Lin-Lin is a person whose life has not been easy.
9. Would you introduce me to the woman who is talking to Tran?
10. We live in Homestead, which has a population of only two.

Practice

Make up some sentences and questions that you could say at a party to get better acquainted with people. Talk about where you are from, how long you have been here, what you do for work and what you do for fun. Be sure your sentences and questions include reflexive naming words. Also be sure to include describing word games that begin with a connecting word.

CHAPTER FIFTEEN

Going on a Trip/Planning

Many people like to use their vacation time to take a trip. The may want to visit friends or relatives who live in another town or region. Or they may want to go someplace with beautiful scenery—like the beach or the mountains—or to an exciting city with many things to see and do. When you are ready to take a vacation trip, here are some things you should know about:

- Making travel arrangements.
- Getting prepared to leave.
- Being a smart tourist.

Making travel arrangements

Your travel arrangements will depend upon several things. First, you need to decide what you want to do during your vacation. You will want to think about how far you must go to get to a place, how much time you have, and how much money you can spend. If you plan to travel a long distance, you will need more time and money. Write down exactly how much money you can spend and mark the days off on a calendar.

How will you get to where you are going? You could drive, fly, ride the bus, or ride the train. Each one has advantages and disadvantages. Again, you will want to think about how far you must go, how much time you have and how much money you can spend.

Driving a car can be the least expensive way to travel. Economy cars give very good mileage, so gas will not cost too much. Driving is also a good way to see the country while traveling. But it can be very tiring if you are traveling a long distance. Also, remember to call your local highway department to check on road conditions. They will

USEFUL WORDS

Action words	Naming words	Describing words
to travel	travel agency/agent	vacancy
to make (a reservation)	tourist	economy
to reserve	transportation	first-class
to inform	representative	sturdy
to arrive	destination	budget
to depart	restricted fare	round-trip
to confirm	lodging	convenient
to list	hotel/motel	single/double
to schedule	taxi	refundable
to pack	bus	nonrefundable
to refund	train	
	airplane	
	route	
	soft-sided luggage	
	carry-on luggage	
	garment bag	

tell you if you should take a different route because of bad weather or road construction.

If you are going to be traveling a long distance alone, you may want to ride the bus. Bus fares are usually reasonable. Call your local bus station for schedule and rate information. Look under "Bus Lines" in the yellow pages. You can compare routes, schedules, and costs to pick the bus line that will best meet your travel needs. Because buses often travel slower than most traffic and make more stops, your travel time will probably be longer if you ride the bus than if you drive.

You can also ride the train. Trains are faster and more comfortable than buses, especially for very long distances. But they cost more. You can call the railroad station or look under "Rail Lines" in the yellow pages to get information on schedules and costs for the train.

Airplanes take you to your destination very quickly, but will cost you more money. It is best to make a reservation for your flight. You can use a travel agency to find the flights that best match your schedule and your budget. (Look under "Travel Agencies and Bureaus" in the yellow pages.) Or you may call the different airlines yourself to see what they have to offer. (Look under "Airline Companies" in the yellow pages.) Most major airlines offer discounted rates if you make a reservation 40 to 70 days before the day you want to leave. Be careful, however, of special offers which may be restricted and nonrefundable. If you are unable to fly for any reason, you won't be able to change your flight plans or get your money back. When you arrive, you may also wish to rent a car from the airport or take a taxicab from the airport to the place you will be staying.

Where will you stay when you arrive at your destination? You will probably need lodging—a place to live for a while. Depending upon where you go, you may choose from a hotel, motel, or bed & breakfast. A hotel offers lodging, meals, entertainment, and personal services, such as room service, laundry, and transportation to and from airports. Because they offer these additional services, hotels cost more than motels. If you want these types of services, you should make sure they are available when you call to reserve a room.

Motels are places that offer lodging and parking. Usually you enter your room directly from an outdoor parking lot. Certain companies run motels with the same name across the whole country. These are called "chains." Most motels and hotels charge for rooms according to how many people stay in the room. One person is "single occupancy," two persons is "double occupancy." Sometimes, children under a certain age are allowed to stay for free. King-sized beds, water beds, and rollaway beds are often an extra charge.

A bed & breakfast inn is located in what is or was once someone's home. You receive a room to sleep in and breakfast in the morning. Breakfast may be "continental," which means coffee, juice, and muffins or biscuits. Since you may get the chance to meet and spend time with the people who live there, staying at a bed & breakfast inn can be very nice. Bed & breakfast inns come in many different prices. Call those located in the area you wish to visit and see if one is in your price range.

Wherever you wish to stay, you should make reservations ahead of time. Then you can be sure there will be a room for you when you arrive. Without a reservation, you will have to watch for a vacancy sign. If the sign says "No Vacancy," then there are no rooms available.

Getting prepared to leave

What will you take with you? Making a list of what you want to take will help you not to forget anything. You will want to think about things like what the weather will be like there, what activities you will do there, and how long you will be there.

If you will be traveling to several different places, then you will want to take only a few pieces of luggage. You may want to take just one piece of luggage. Otherwise, you will have to deal with the problems of packing, unpacking, and carrying many bags. So pack only those things you will not be able to buy when you get there and cannot do without. You can buy trial-size containers of shampoo, conditioner, toothpaste, mouthwash, and other toiletries. This will save space in your suitcase or traveling bag.

If you will stay in one place for a long time, then you may pack extra things in a large suitcase. If you are using public transportation, you may have to pay more for extra baggage. Call the airline company, bus company, or train company to find out the details.

Pack those things you cannot do without. If you are taking a special medication, then you will want to check with your doctor and get the prescription filled ahead of time. Pack these in a special place with any important medical information.

Who will take care of things while you are away? You could ask a friend to water your plants and take care of your pets. Places where you may leave pets overnight for a fee are listed in the yellow pages under "Pet Boarding" or "Kennels." If you will be gone a long time, then you may want the post office to hold your mail until you return. Call the subscription department of the newspaper if you want them to hold delivery of your paper until you return.

It is most important that your home or apartment does not look empty. People are less likely to disturb your home if it looks like you are there. A light may be left on outside at night. If you live in a house, then you may want to tell your neighbors how long you will be away. If you live in an apartment, tell your apartment manager when you will be gone. These people can make sure nothing unusual happens to your home.

All appliances that will not be used while you are gone should be unplugged. Unplug the toaster, blender, microwave, iron, television, lamps, etc. But do *not* unplug the refrigerator. Windows should be closed and locked. Curtains and shades should be closed so no one can see into your home. If you have an answering machine on your telephone, you may want to leave it turned off, unless someone will check your messages regularly.

Being a smart tourist

There are several things you may do to have the best vacation you can imagine. Cities and places that attract many tourists can be fun. These places can also be hectic and dangerous. Here are some tips on how to be a smart tourist:

• Use traveler's checks to protect against your money being stolen. No one can spend a traveler's check but the person who bought it. Also, if traveler's checks are lost, they can be replaced at little or no cost.

• Tour cities on special tour buses. This is the easiest and quickest way to get an overall view of cities you are visiting. Then you can decide which places you want to take a closer look at later in your trip.

• Look for discounts and bargains to help you save money. Sometimes it is easy to ask the local people of the area for more information on good deals. Certain part of town may be well known for variety of merchandise and bargain prices. You will probably find these areas to be full of interesting and unusual people as well. Don't be afraid to discover the real personality of a city!

MAKING RESERVATIONS: A SAMPLE CONVERSATION

Alfonso and Maria Fuentes plan to visit Disney World on their vacation. They will drive to Orlando, Florida, where Disney World is located, but they are not sure what time they will arrive. They want to stay in a motel that is nice but reasonably priced. Marie finds a toll-free number of a motel chain in the yellow pages. She calls to make a reservation.

Woman: Worldwide reservations. May I help you?

Maria: Hello. I'm calling to make reservations for February 13th and 14th.

Woman: What city, ma'am?

Maria: Orlando, Florida, please.

Woman: Yes, ma'am. We have four motels in Orlando. The Airport Motel, the Downtown Motel, the Disney World Motel, and the Interstate Motel. Do you have a preference?

Maria: Yes, we'd like the Disney World Motel, if possible.

Woman: Certainly. How many people will be staying?

Maria: Me and my husband. That's two.

Woman: All right, double occupancy. Do you want a room with a king-sized bed or two double beds?

Maria: My goodness, I never thought of that! Well, a king-sized bed might be nice. Does it cost more?

Woman: Two doubles cost $40 and one king-sized costs $45.

Maria: Well, we don't need to spend $5 just for a king-sized bed. We'll just take the two double beds.

Woman: That's fine, ma'am. Now, please tell me again the nights you will be staying.

Maria: February 13th and 14th.

Woman: Two nights. Okay. Now, when will you be arriving?

Maria: I'm not sure. We're going to drive and I don't know how long the drive will be or how early we'll be able to leave.

Woman: Do you want to guarantee your reservation for late arrival?

Maria: I'm sorry, I don't understand what you mean.

Woman: If you think you will arrive after 6 P.M., you can guarantee that your room will still be reserved. You just have to give me a credit card number. Otherwise, the motel manager may think you have broken your reservation and he might give your room to someone else.

Maria: Oh, I'm pretty sure we'll be there before 6 P.M. I don't think we need to guarantee our reservation.

Woman: That's fine, ma'am. Now, may I have your name and address, please?

Maria: Maria and Alfonso Fuentes. We live at 3367 Willow Court in Atlanta, Georgia.

Woman: Let me confirm this information, Mrs. Fuentes. You want a double occupancy room at the Disney World Motel for the nights of February 13th and 14th. Is that correct?

Maria: Yes.

Woman: Your room is reserved. Thank you for staying at our motel.

Maria: Thank you.

USING A TRAVEL AGENT

A travel agent is a person who sells and arranges transportation, trips, and tours for travelers. Travel agents have all kinds of information about different vacations—including different kinds of transportation (air travel, bus tours, train trips, cruises on ships, and so on), different kinds of lodging (hotels, beach cabins, wilderness lodges, and so on), and different kinds of activities (mountain climbing, visiting museums and places of historic interest, seeing performances of music, dance, and theater, and so on). Travel agents arrange for group rates and find discounts that the general public may not know about.

A travel agent can give you as much or as little help with your travel plans as you want. Many people use travel agents only to purchase airline tickets, because this service is free and convenient. The travel agent has flight schedules and rate information for all the major airlines on a computer. He or she can sell you the best-priced ticket available and at the same time find the flight time that best suits your needs. If you want to take a "package" vacation, you can ask a travel agent to set you up with transportation and lodging at a nice resort or in an exciting city. Some packages even include tickets to shows or museums and some meals at restaurants.

GETTING READY TO GO: A SAMPLE CONVERSATION

It is Wednesday evening. Maria and Alfonso are taking care of last-minute preparations for their trip, which begins in three days.

Alfonso: Maria, did you talk to Rhonda next door about watching Lobo?

Maria: Yes, she said she will be glad to take care of him. I showed her where we keep the dog food and how much food to put in his bowl. She said her nephews are coming to visit her next week, so Lobo will have someone to play with.

Alfonso: Ah, that's good. I feel bad leaving poor Lobo by himself for so long. Did you already give Rhonda a key?

Maria: No, I'll give it to her on Friday before we leave. Oh yes, I asked her to take care of our mail, too.

Alfonso: Why? I thought you were going to tell the post office to hold it until we get back?

Maria: I thought that was a lot of trouble for just one week. Rhonda will be coming over here every day anyway. It won't be any trouble for her to bring in the mail and put it on the coffee table.

Alfonso: You're right. That will be much simpler. Well, I called the newspaper today and told them to stop delivery until the Sunday we return.

Maria: Good. I'll check that off on our list of "Things to Do." Let's see . . . what is on the list that still needs to be done? The tires, the laundry, and your prescription.

Alfonso: Tomorrow I'm taking the car to the garage. I decided to get a quick check-over, just in case. I'll have them rotate the tires, too. And I think I'll get another used tire to have for a spare. I want to make sure we don't have any serious trouble on the road!

Maria: That will put my mind at rest, Al. I worry when we drive so far.

Alfonso: We'll do fine on this trip, *querida mía*. Don't worry!

Maria: Okay, okay. Back to the list! I will do all of the laundry on Thursday night. That's tomorrow! Oh, Alfonso, I'm getting excited! Now, what about getting your allergy prescription refilled? Do you want me to go by the drugstore or will you?

Alfonso: I'll be tied up at the garage tomorrow, and Friday we've got to finish packing. I know you've got to do the laundry tomorrow, but could you find time to go to the drugstore?

Maria: Sure, I can do it. There are probably a few other things I need to pick up there, anyway. Oh! That just reminded me—I keep thinking we need to put a first-aid kit in the car! But I always

AUTO TRAVEL CLUB

Auto travel clubs provide many services for their members. You can become a member for a certain amount of money per year. Most travel clubs, such as the the American Automobile Association, or AAA, provide automobile services such as:

- Lockout service (in case you lock your keys in your car).
- Towing (in case your car won't run for some reason).
- Emergency road service and repair.
- Battery check and recharge.
- Guidebooks with travel and tourist information.
- "Triptiks," detailed maps showing the exact route to follow on a particular trip.

AAA can also tell you about road conditions. As a member, you can go to the AAA office and tell them your driving destination. Your AAA representative will prepare a special package just for your trip. The package may include state maps, a city or state guidebook, and a triptik. Look up automobile clubs under "Associations" in the yellow pages of your telephone book.

forget to write it down on my list. I will get a kit at the drugstore when I get your prescription.

Alfonso: How could you survive without your lists, Maria?

Maria (laughing): I don't know, Al! But I'm certain we could never get anything done without them!

Alfonso: I believe you are right, *querida mía*. You are so organized. We could never get all these preparations finished before our vacation if you didn't have everything under control.

LANGUAGE SKILLS

Most trips need to be carefully ***planned*** so that all the details are taken care of. Then you can just relax and enjoy your vacation! Here are some important language skills you need in order to make ***plans:***

- How to use action words to talk about things to do.
- How to use connecting words to talk about different choices.

Using Action Words

Sometimes action words act like naming words in sentences. Instead of telling what happened, these action words name a *situation* or an *activity* (which are *things*). Most of the time, the action word is part of a word group. Here are some examples of action words and word groups used as naming words:

Examples: *Traveling by air* is the fastest way to get there.
Planning carefully will make your trip more fun.
Moti enjoyed *dancing* every night on his vacation.
The best part of our trip was *photographing the animals*.

When action words are used as naming words, they usually end in **-ing**. These action/naming words can come before the action word in the sentence or after it. Let's study two of the examples that were given above:

Traveling by air is the fastest way to get there.

- **Traveling by air** is the action/naming word group.
- **is** is the action word.
- **the fastest way to get there** is a describing word group that tells about air travel.

Moti enjoyed dancing every night on his vacation.

- **Moti** is the naming word.
- **enjoyed** is the action word.
- **dancing** is the action/naming word that tells what Moti enjoyed.
- **every night on his vacation** is the describing word grop that tells when Moti enjoyed dancing.

When action words are used as naming words, they sometimes take the basic **to** form: *to walk, to ride, to see*. Here are a few examples of these action/naming words and word groups:

Examples: *To see the pyramids* has been my lifelong dream.
We are going *to hike in the national forest*.

Here is a closer look at these two sentences:

To see the pyramids has been my lifelong dream.

- **To see the pyramids** is the action/naming word group.
- **has been** is the action word.
- **my lifelong dream** is the describing word group.

We are going to hike in the national forest.

- **We** is the naming word.
- **are going** is the action word.
- **to hike in the national forest** is the action/naming word group.

TO LEARN MORE ABOUT ACTION WORDS, STUDY CHAPTER 18.
TO LEARN MORE ABOUT NAMING WORDS, STUDY CHAPTER 17.

Exercise 15.1

In the space provided in each sentence, turn the action word into an action/naming word by adding **-ing** to the end. The first sentence has been done for you. (The answer key is on page 191.)

Note: When an action word ends with the letter *e*, drop the *e* before adding *-ing*.

Examples: *ride, riding . . . make, making*

1. **[See]** <u>Seeing</u> the wild animals was the best part of our trip to Africa.
2. We had as much fun **[plan]** ______________ our trip as we had **[take]** ______________ it.
3. **[Go]** ______________ to the beach is her favorite activity.
4. He enjoyed **[develop]** ______________ his own film after the trip.
5. Marta helped Cosimo with his **[pack]** ______________.

Exercise 15.2

Underline the action/naming word group in these sentences. Then rewrite the sentence using the other action/naming word form. The first sentence has been done for you. (The answer key is on page 191.)

1. <u>To ride all night in the bus</u> is the way to get an early start.

   <u>Riding all night in the bus is the way to get an early start.</u>

2. Lying in the sun on a tropical beach is my idea of a great vacation.

   ____

3. Listening to calypso music reminds me of my trip to Jamaica.

   ____

4. To see the Matterhorn would be fun!

   ____

5. Sleeping in my hammock is how I want to spend my vacation.

   ____

Using Connecting Words

Certain connecting words are used to talk about things that are *possible* but not *actual.* These connecting words are **if, as if,** and **as though**. The action word **were** appears later in the sentence. Often the action word **would** appears as well. Here are some examples that show how these connecting words show possibility:

Examples: *If* we *were* to visit Paris, we *would* not have time for Rome.
They *would* never have met *if* she *were* not on that plane.
It is *as if* we never left.
Lana slept *as if* she *were* dead.
I remember that cafe *as though* I *were* there only yesterday.
We felt *as though* we *were* gone forever.

These example sentences talk about situations or actions that are *not true*, although they are possible:

They would never have met if *she were not on that plane* . . . but she was on that plane and they did meet.

Lana slept as if *she were dead* . . . but she was not dead, she only looked that way in her sleep.

I remember that cafe as though *I were there only yesterday* . . . but I was not there yesterday, I just remember it clearly.

TO LEARN MORE ABOUT CONNECTING WORDS, STUDY CHAPTER 20.

Exercise 15.3

Some of these sentences are correct, but some use the *wrong* words to talk about something that is possible. If a sentence is correct, write "okay" in the space beside it. If it is incorrect, write the *correct* word or words in the space. The first one has been done for you. (The answer key is on page 191.)

_If_ 1. **As if** I were to take the tour bus, I might not return in time to have dinner with you.
____2. She acts **as though** she has never seen a Frenchman before.
____3. Jerry would come with us **as though** he could get the time off from work.
____4. We would be too early **if** we were to leave now.
____5. Carmen and Miguel act **if** they want to extend their trip another month.

____6. **As though** you were to leave the umbrella, it would surely rain cats and dogs!

____7. We felt **as if** we had been gone for two years instead of just two weeks.

____8. The customs inspector would not have let us through **if** we were not carrying our passports.

Practice

Make up sentences that tell about a trip you once took or a trip you would like to take. Talk about your travel arrangements and what you did to prepare for your trip. Then tell about the things you saw and did while you were away. Be sure to use sentences with action/naming words. Also talk about things that were *possible*, but did not actually happen.

CHAPTER SIXTEEN

Using Government and Community Services/Insisting

In this country, different government offices provide many services. For example, they help unemployed people find jobs, give poor people money, build and repair roads and hospitals, give licenses for driving or getting married, and enforce the law. Also, some services are provided by nongovernment community agencies. Some of these agencies are paid by the government to help people; others get money from donations and fees. Even if you are not a citizen of this country, you have the right to use these services. This chapter gives you information about how to deal with these organizations:

- Getting information.
- Finding help.
- Making complaints.

Getting information

The ***telephone book*** is a good resource for much information. You may be able to find everything you need in some part of the telephone book. You can find the following information:

- A list of helpful numbers.
- City government office telephone numbers.
- Regional government office telephone numbers.
- National government office telephone numbers.

Regional and national government office numbers also are listed in alphabetical order.

USEFUL WORDS

Action words	Naming words	Describing words
to request	resource	nonprofit
to insist	reference	alphabetical order
to perform, to do	interference	social service
to report	utilities	public
to prevent	pollution	private
to recycle	waste management	
to repair	consumer	
to counsel, to get counseling	authorities	
	government	
to refer	agency	
to assist, to help	department	
	bureau	
	board	
	commission	

These offices have various names, such as department, division, commission, bureau, board, and agency. Some of these offices are run by government officials and some are paid for with government money. Usually, city and regional governments have one number to call for information. The operator who answers can tell you which department you should call, depending upon what you want.

The ***yellow pages*** include business and organization telephone numbers listed according to the service they offer or the matter they are concerned with. You will find all the private and nonprofit social service organizations listed there. For example, hospitals and various health organizations are listed in alphabetical order under "Health Agencies" in the yellow pages. Different community centers, rehabilitation and treatment centers, child and family services groups, and citizen organizations are just some of the many numbers listed under "Social Service Organizations."

The ***public library*** is another valuable resource. Many public libraries have a number to call for specific information on any subject. Usually, the operator will call you back with an answer to your question or several book titles where you might find what you need. The public library can provide information on a wide range of subjects. Although you usually need a library card to check out books, anyone may go to the library and use its services there.

Many government, nongovernment, and nonprofit agencies publish pamphlets, handbooks, newspapers, and magazines. These are usually available at your public library.

Finding help

You may need to get help for any number of problems. Sometimes the problem is an emergency—like a serious accident, a fire, a life-threatening illness or injury, a burglary, or a rape. Your telephone book has a list of emergency numbers for the fire department, police, sheriff, and ambulance. Other emergency numbers, such as the Crisis Intervention Hotline and the Poison Control Center, are also located in the front of the phone book.

Most problems are not emergencies. However, they can be just as serious and important.

Below is a list of areas in which people often have problems that they need help to solve. By looking in the telephone book, you can find organizations that can help you solve problems like these.

Children. Many people need help in taking care of their children. If both parents work, they need day care for their young ones. If a child doesn't have a father or mother (or just needs more caring adults in his or her life), then organizations like Big Brothers/Big Sisters can help. So can youth organizations and centers like the YMCA and the Boys Club.

Counseling. Sometimes people need someone to talk to, a counselor who is trained to help them deal with their feelings and make important decisions. When people have problems with rebellious children, arguing families, alcohol or drug abuse, physical or sexual abuse, or rape, they can get help from many different counseling services.

Disabled. People who have a physical problem—they are blind, deaf, retarded, or wheelchair-bound—need help in many different ways. They may need special health care and special educational help. They may need help getting around town or getting chores done. They might even need special equipment in their houses, like telephones for the deaf. All of these services are available.

Elderly. Older people have many of the same problems as children and disabled people. Perhaps they need a place to be looked after during the day. Many need help with food, chores, and health care. They can get help from organizations that bring hot meals to older people at home. They can also get help from errand and driving services.

Health. Health problems trouble many people. Some people have diseases that take a long time to cure—or may never be cured. There are organizations that give people information and support to deal with these diseases. To give people access to health care, certain clinics offer their services for free or for a much smaller fee than usual. Also, the government offers medical welfare payments to people who qualify.

Housing. People sometimes need help in finding a place to live that they can afford. They also may need help in getting their landlords to take proper care of their homes. Sometimes bad roofs and floors, broken plumbing and appliances, and other dangerous or unhealthy conditions are not repaired. Tenants can find help from both government and nonprofit organizations.

Legal. Sometimes people need help in dealing with the law. They may have been accused of a crime, or they may have been the victim of a crime. People can get free or inexpensive legal help from legal-aid organizations.

Shelters. People sometimes face the problem of having no place to stay. They may not have a home at all. Or they may need to leave their homes because they are in danger there. Women and children who are being hurt by their husbands, fathers, or boyfriends can find a shelter that will protect them for a while. Homeless people can also find places to stay for days, weeks, or months until they can find a real home.

Financial support. From time to time, people simply may not have enough money to take care of themselves and their families. The government provides welfare money to help people meet their basic needs. Also, people who have lost their jobs might be able to get unemployment money from the government. Many nonprofit and church charities also help with food, clothing, housing, and money. There are organizations that offer used clothing and household items at very low cost, sometimes even for free.

Making complaints

Public services are things that must be done to keep the city or county up to certain standards of safety and health. These services are offered to the public on a regular basis. Some of these services are provided without any request from citizens. Other services are performed when a citizen or group of citizens requests action. Here are examples of some public services and times when you might need to request action:

- Traffic departments carry out street and bridge repair. They put up and repair street signs and traffic lights. Dangerous roadways should be reported to the traffic department.

• Animal problems or concerns should be reported to animal control. Dead animals should be reported to animal control. The animal or humane society (dog pound) houses lost and stray animals. If your cat or dog is missing, you'll want to check with the animal shelter.

• Garbage pickup is a public service performed by the city or private waste management companies. Some buildings have large Dumpsters where trash may be deposited. Other places, including most private homes, are part of a garbage route. One or two days a week, a garbage truck will drive by and pick up any garbage left out. Garbage can be stored in paper bags, plastic bags, metal or plastic garbage cans.

Glass, newspapers, and aluminum recycling services are now available in many cities. Glass, newspapers, and aluminum should be separated from other trash and garbage. They may then be left in marked containers at self-service recycling centers. Some cities also have recycling service routes. On certain days of the week, glass, newspapers, and aluminum will be picked up in front of your house.

• Noise, air, and water pollution make the environment dirty, unsafe, and just plain unpleasant. Man-made waste is usually the problem. Some places have laws against littering and will punish persons who litter. The punishment may be a fine of a certain amount of money or time spent in jail. If you see someone littering, you should report him or her to the proper authorities.

• Unsafe locations are usually marked with a warning sign. These areas include abandoned buildings, unfenced junkyards, unfenced pits, etc. Areas such as these that are not marked should be reported immediately to the police. Children are often hurt while playing in such areas.

MAKING A COMPLAINT: A SAMPLE CONVERSATION

Sako Zendar is sitting on his front porch. He hurt his back at his job a few weeks ago and cannot return to work for several months. His neighbor Amar has come by to visit him.

Amar: Sako, are you doing okay?
Sako: I am feeling better, Amar, but there is still a lot of pain. I'm just glad to be able to move around a little bit.

As the men sit talking, a very loud car drives past the house.

Amar: Can you believe that? He was flying through that intersection! I bet he was going over the speed limit! He should be arrested.
Sako: Yeah, but he didn't have a stop sign.
Amar: But he was speeding, Sako. If there had been any little children, they might be dead now.
Sako: I know.
Amar: What are we going to do, Sako? There are many little children in our neighborhood. When the high school lets out, those teenage kids always drive by here too fast. How could they see a little child getting ready to cross the street?
Sako: There should be a stop sign there. That certainly would slow them down.
Amar: You're right, Sako. We need a stop sign at that corner. I wonder who we should talk to about that. Who is in charge of stop signs anyway? I guess it would be a department in the city government.
Sako: Let's look in the phone book to see what we can find. Will you go get mine? It's by the telephone.

Amar walks in the house to get the telephone book. Then he walks out onto the porch again. He and Sako look at the telephone book together.

Amar: Here we go. Let's look under government offices.
Sako: Okay. Hmm, there's a number called "Emergency Road Condition." I guess this isn't really an emergency. And there are several numbers listed under "Highways and Public Transportation." But they are for things like getting permits and finding out travel information. None of those are what we are looking for.
Amar: Under "Streets" they have a number for street repair. That's not what we want either.
Sako: Well, let's look in the section for city offices.
Amar: Look at all the different departments!

"Building Inspection" . . . "Health Department" . . . "Parks and Recreation Department" . . . "Police Department." None of those would have anything to do with roads.
Sako: Look! How about "Transportation and Public Services Department"? That might be the one. Why don't we at least call and find out. If they don't take care of stop signs, maybe they can tell us who does.
Amar: Good idea. Let's call now. I'd like to get that stop sign up as quickly as we can.
Sako: It's good to know that I can still do *something*, even though I can't get around very well!

GETTING INFORMATION: A SAMPLE CONVERSATION

Srah is Sako's wife. She and Helena, another neighbor, are talking in her kitchen one afternoon.
Srah: Now that Sako can't go to work, I have twice as much work to do around the house. He is in so much pain and I feel so sorry for him. Still, he doesn't have to be so mean to me sometimes.
Helena: Does he hurt you?
Srah: Oh, no, he is just very grumpy. I wish he would just be quiet sometimes! And I am worried about Mantaal, too. He just turned twelve. We had a birthday party for him and he didn't even care. He didn't want to have any of his friends there. He won't talk to me anymore. And I know he doesn't talk to his father. I am so worried about him, Helena.
Helena: Does he have any friends?
Srah: I don't even know. I don't know what to do about this. Everything seems to be going wrong at the same time. I just wish there was someone I could talk to about it. Sako doesn't know what to do. Mantaal's grades are very poor. He won't study when I tell him to. I just don't know.
Helena: Srah, I know there are people who can help you. You should look for help.
Srah: But we don't have any money, Helena. Sako is getting some insurance money because of his back, but we must watch every dollar. We can't afford to pay for something extra.
Helena: Most of these service organizations are for people just like you, Srah. They know that people sometimes need help when they can't afford it. They give help for free, or else they ask for only a little money. Come on, let's look in the telephone book to see what kinds of help you might be able to get. It won't hurt to just look!
Srah: Okay. You are right. Maybe I will learn something.
Helena: Let's look in the yellow pages. I'll look under the heading "Social Service Organizations." Here it is.
Srah: What is listed here?
Helena: Well, how about some counseling? There are several counseling centers listed here.
Srah: What is counseling?
Helena: Counselors help people figure out what is bothering them and find solutions. You could talk to a counselor about Mantaal. Or you could take Mantaal to a counselor. Maybe the counselor could help you find out why Mantaal is having such a hard time right now and how you can help him get through it.
Srah: I'm not sure Sako would like talking to a stranger. But I know he is worried about Mantaal, too. I think he would like to help, but he doesn't know how. Maybe he would talk to someone if he thought it would really help Mantaal.
Helena: Oh, Srah, here is a group I've heard of before. It's called Big Brothers/Big Sisters. These are adults who volunteer to spend time with youngsters. It is a very well-known organization. I think you should call to find out all the details. It might be just right for Mantaal.
Srah: You know, that might be just what Mantaal needs. Some different activities might give him the chance to meet some new friends.
Helena: New friends. That's a good idea. Let me think . . . where could he meet other kids his age? I'll look under "Youth" here in the yellow pages. Let's see . . . here's "Youth Organizations and Centers." There is the Boys Club and the YMCA. Those are also well-known places with lots of activities for children. Why don't you call and see what they offer.
Srah: Helena, thank you so much. I feel better already just knowing that there are some places I can go for help.

LANGUAGE SKILLS

When you are dealing with government offices and community organizations, sometimes you will talk to people who are not very concerned about your wants and needs. Perhaps they are too busy. Maybe they don't want to go to the trouble. Perhaps they are more concerned with following rules than with helping you. Unfortunately, situations like these come up everywhere in the world. To deal with people like this, you must know how to ***insist***. If you do not give up, often your requests for help will be met. Here are two important language skills you need in order to ***insist*** or convince people to do what you ask:

- How to use helping words to insist.
- How to use connecting words to make a convincing argument.

Using Helping Words

One way to insist that something be done is to use the helping words **must** and **must not** with an action word.

Examples: You *must return* my call before 5 P.M. today.
She *must not forget* to leave a message for him.
Someone *must check* on this as soon as possible.

Sometimes we use a form of the words **have** and **be** after the words **must** and **must not** and before an action word.

Examples: You *must not have corrected* the problem.
I *must have* an answer today.
This *must be taken* care of immediately.
This matter *must not be avoided* any longer.

Exercise 16.1

Here are some sentences requesting or suggesting some kind of action. Change them to insist that the action take place. Use the words **must** or **must not** in your new sentence. The first one has been done for you. (The answer key is on page 191.)

1. They should fix the toilet before the weekend. ___They must fix the toilet before the weekend.___

____

2. We could stay in the shelter until we find jobs. _______________________

____

3. The garbage is ready to be picked up. _______________________

____

4. My neighbor should be told that his dog should be on a leash. _______________________

____

5. We need to know what to do right away. _______________________

____

6. We cannot let people drive too fast on this street. ______________________________

____

7. The city will not let these tree branches damage the electric lines. ______________________________

____

8. I need the stop sign put up so my children can play safely. ______________________________

____

9. You should call a legal-aid society for help with that crooked loan company. ______________________________

____

10. We do not have to put up with this trouble. ______________________________

____

TO LEARN MORE ABOUT ACTION WORDS, STUDY CHAPTER 18.

Using Connecting Words

Some connecting words help to go from one thought to another. These words express authority and are often used to make a convincing argument:

as a result	for example	in fact
in other words	as well as	after all
finally	eventually	however
otherwise	next	instead
also	besides	

Sometimes these connecting words help to further explain something you have already been talking about.

Examples: The living-room carpet is very wet *as a result* of the toilet problem.
In fact, the carpet is ruined and must be replaced.

Sometimes these words let your audience know you are about to conclude or give a sense of time to your description.

Examples: *Finally,* someone must look at this problem.
After I called four times, the plumber *finally* looked at the toilet.

TO LEARN MORE ABOUT CONNECTING WORDS, STUDY CHAPTER 20.

Exercise 16.2

Each of the following exercises has two sentences. One of the two sentences uses a connecting word or phrase. Underline the connecting word or words. The first one has been done for you. (The answer key is on page 191.)

1. I must have an answer today. After all, I have been waiting for three weeks to hear from your office.
2. Eventually the roof caved in. It could not withstand the weight of the snow.
3. The manager told me to leave instead of asking me in a nice manner. I am very upset.

4. The man who visited my house said he would make the call. Otherwise, I would have called.
5. The toilet drips, won't flush, and smells horrible. In other words, it is broken and must be repaired.
6. The utility man said they would check into the problem right away. However, I haven't heard a word from them.
7. We are concerned about the safety of our neighborhood as well as the high taxes we pay. The city just isn't doing its job.
8. The first thing we must do is call for information. Next, we must form a neighborhood committee.
9. Juana should not have to pay for the roof to be repaired. After all, she is only renting the house.

Practice

Pretend your friend is the person you must speak with about what you need. Tell your friend not to give you what you need unless she is convinced by your argument. Explain your problem using helping words to insist or to convince your friend to do what you ask. Be assertive. Describe the situation that has caused your problem or need. Use connecting words to make a convincing argument.

PART TWO

CHAPTER SEVENTEEN

Using Words That Name People, Places, and Things

Naming words are the most common words in English. There are two basic kinds of naming words: regular naming words (called *nouns*) and substitute naming words (called *pronouns*).

NAMING WORDS: NOUNS

Proper or common

Nouns can be ***proper*** or ***common***. A *proper* naming word tells the *actual name* of a person, place, or thing. A *common* naming word is a general word for a person, place, or thing. Here are some examples:

Proper	***Common***
George Washington	man
Canada	country
English	language
Christmas	holiday
Main Street	street

Number

Naming words must show ***number***. In other words, they must show whether you are talking about *one* (called *singular*) or *more than one* (called *plural*) person, place, or thing. Most naming words add the **-s, -z,** or **-ez** to show *more than one*. The sound is written as **s** or **es**. Here are some examples:

One	***More than one***
week	weeks
home	homes
dollar	dollars
handshake	handshakes
hope	hopes

Some naming words change in different ways when they go from one to more than one. Here are some examples of words that do not follow the rule:

One	***More than one***
leaf	leaves
wife	wives
foot	feet
mouse	mice
child	children

Some naming words do not show number. However, you can combine them with other naming words that *do* show number. Here are some examples:

Naming word	***One***	***More than one***
sunlight	*ray* of sunlight	*rays* of sunlight
butter	*stick* of butter	*sticks* of butter
scissors	*pair* of scissors	*pairs* of scissors
cloth	*piece* of cloth	*pieces* of cloth
milk	*glass* of milk	*glasses* of milk

Some naming words can be combined with other words that show ***quantity*** (how much) instead of number (how many). Here are some examples of words that show quantity:

Naming word	***General amount***
soup	*can* of soup
perfume	*bottle* of perfume
detergent	*box* of detergent
ointment	*jar* of ointment
bread	*loaf* of bread
toothpaste	*tube* of toothpaste

Belonging

Naming words can be changed to show that something belongs to the person, place, or thing that has been named. When these naming words are changed to show *belonging*, they are called ***possessive.*** Naming words usually add the sound **-s, -z,** or **-ez** to show belonging. The sound usually is written as **'s** or **s'**. Sometimes it is shown just with **'**.

Belonging means several different things. Here are some examples to show you these different meanings:

- *Owning*: Albert's car (the car is owned by Albert)
  baby's shoes (the shoes are owned by the baby)
- *Making:* students' presentation (the presentation was made by the students)
  Lim's poem (the poem was made by Lim)
- *Giving:* father's permission (permission was given by the father)
  teacher's praise (praise was given by the teacher)
- *Using:* girls' bathroom (the bathroom is used by girls)
  Mary's desk (the desk is used by Mary)
- *Having:* doctor's appointment (the appointment is had with the doctor)
  enemy's hatred (the hatred is had by the enemy)

When something belongs to *one person*, add the sound of **-s, -z,** or **-ez**. When it belongs to *more than one* person, usually you do not need to add the sound. It usually was already added when the naming word was changed from one (singular) to more than one (plural). Here are some examples:

One	***More than one***
teacher's class	teachers' classes
store's sale	stores' sales
building's windows	buildings' windows
cat's toys	cats' toys

Note: In writing, possessive form is shown as **'s** when talking about one person, place, or thing. It is shown as **s'** when talking about more than one person, place, or thing.

SUBSTITUTE NAMING WORDS: PRONOUNS

Personal pronouns

Certain substitute naming words are used in place of *specific* proper or common nouns. These are called ***personal pronouns***. There are seven groups of personal pronouns. Each group has different pronouns for different uses. Here are the seven groups of pronouns:

I, me, my, mine	you, your, yours
he, him, his	we, us, our, ours
she, her, hers	they, them, their, theirs
it, its	

The personal pronoun you should use depends upon the answers to these questions:

- *Whom are you referring to?* In English grammar, this is called the ***person***. There are three types of person. Each type has different groups of pronouns:

  First person: You are referring to yourself.
  I, me, my, mine
  we, us, our, ours

  Second person: You are referring to the person, place, or thing you are talking *to*.
  you, your, yours

  Third person: You are referring to the person, place, or thing you are talking *about*.
  he, him, his
  she, her, hers
  it, its
  they, them, their, theirs

• *How many are you referring to?* Like nouns, personal pronouns show ***number***. Here are the groups of pronouns according to number:

One	***More than one***
I, me, my, mine	we, us, our, ours
you, your, yours	you, your, yours
he, him, his	they, them, their, theirs
she, her, hers	
it, its	

• *Are you referring to a male, a female, or something that is neither?* In English, the word ***gender*** refers to this quality. Here are the pronouns that specifically refer to the gender of the person or thing that is named:

Male: he, him, his
Female: she, her, hers

The personal pronouns that are not included in these lists do not show gender at all. They can be used for any gender.

• *Are you referring to someone or something that is doing an action?* In sentences, the person, place, or thing that is doing the action is called the ***subject***. The subject is usually at the beginning of a sentence. Here are the personal pronouns that are in *subject form*:

I: *I* ran in the race.
You: *You* made a pie.
He: *He* asked for my phone number.
She: *She* has thirty pairs of shoes.
It: *It* broke into a dozen pieces.
We: *We* cannot find the tickets.
They: *They* laughed at the movie.

• *Are you referring to someone or something that is receiving an action?* In sentences, the person, place, or thing that is receiving the action of the subject is called the ***object***. The object is usually after the action word in a sentence. Here are the personal pronouns that are in *object form:*

Me: The policeman gave *me* a warning.
You: I saw *you* in the store.
Him: The boss gave *him* a big raise.
Her: Lee called *her* a liar.
It: They tore *it* down years ago.
Us: The storm blew *us* down the street.
Them: The truck hit *them* from behind.

• *Are you referring to someone or something that "possesses" another person, place, or thing?* Like nouns, personal pronouns can show belonging. These pronouns are ***possessive***. There are two kinds of possessive pronouns: *possessive subject pronouns* and *possessive object pronouns:*

Possessive subject pronouns

My: *My* arm is sore.
Your: *Your* home looks new.
His: *His* friend left town.
Her: *Her* car won't start.
Its: *Its* roof is full of leaks.

Our: *Our* trip begins tomorrow.
Their: *Their* knowledge is limited.

Possessive object pronouns
Mine: Kim's hair is shorter than *mine*.
Yours: We think this ring might be *yours*.
His: Neem said the cake was *his*.
Hers: If the scarf is pink, it is *hers*.
Ours: The last house on the right is *ours*.
Theirs: The picture is either hers or *theirs*.

- *Are you referring to someone or something that is referring to itself?* These pronouns are called ***reflexive***, because they reflect back to the subject of the sentence.

Myself: I felt ashamed of *myself.*
(*Myself* reflects back on *I*.)
Yourself: How can you stand to look at *yourself?*
(*Yourself* reflects back on *you*.)
Himself: José seemed very proud of *himself.*
(*Himself* reflects back on *José*.)
Herself: She smiled at *herself* in the mirror.
(*Herself* reflects back on *she*.)
Itself: The house of cards fell in on *itself.*
(*Itself* reflects back on *the house of cards*.)
Ourselves: We should give *ourselves* a vacation this year.
(*Ourselves* reflects back on *we*.)
Themselves: The girls are trying to keep up with *themselves.*
(*Themselves* reflects back on the *girls*.)

Indefinite pronouns

Certain pronouns are *general* words that can substitute for nouns or personal pronouns. These are called ***indefinite pronouns*** because they do not refer to a specific person, place, or thing. Here is a list of indefinite pronouns.

other	another	some
anybody	anyone	anything
everybody	everyone	everything
nobody	no one	nothing
somebody	someone	something
both	none	several

Use indefinite pronouns when you do not want or need to name a *particular* person, place, or thing. Also use them when you do not want or need to use a personal pronoun.

Naming word	***Personal pronoun***	***Indefinite pronoun***
Nancy screamed.	*She* screamed.	*Someone* screamed.
Aziz, Louis, and Ting asked questions.	*They* asked questions.	*Several* asked questions.
The group started laughing.	*We* started laughing.	*Everyone* started laughing.

Some indefinite pronouns refer to *one* person, place or thing. Others refer to *more than one*. Some can refer to *either* one or more than one.

One person, place, or thing: another, anybody, anyone, anything, everybody, everyone, everything, nobody, no one, nothing, somebody, someone, something.

Examples: We found two yesterday and *another* today.
Can *anybody* find the answer to this question?
Anyone can apply for a scholarship.
Don't do *anything* until I get there.
Is *everybody* happy?
Make sure *everyone* is in the picture.
Everything went wrong today.
Nobody noticed the leak.
No one wants to go to the movie with me.
Nothing important was discussed at the meeting.
Somebody will have to pay for the damages.
Someone called while you were out.
Something smells bad in the garbage.

More than one person, place, or thing: both, some.

Examples: I have two brothers. *Both* are coming to visit.
All jobs are not equal. *Some* are better than others.

Either one or more than one person, place, or thing: other, none.

Examples: Some of us wanted to keep going. *Others* wanted to rest first.
They all enjoyed the movie. But *none* liked the restaurant.
There are several movies playing. *None* are ones I want to see.
One of the telephones is here. The *other* is in the bedroom.

Demonstrative pronouns

Certain substitute naming words are used to show how near or far a person, place, or thing is. These words are called ***demonstrative*** because they demonstrate (or show) distance in space and time. Demonstrative pronouns can be used alone, or they can be used together with a naming word (noun). Here are the demonstrative pronouns:

- **This** refers to *one* thing that is *near* to you in space or time.
  Examples: *This* looks like a good steak.
  This is the first meat I have eaten in a week.
- **These** refers to *more than one* thing that is *near* to you in space or time.
  Examples: *These* are the boxes I got to move with.
  These days I don't mind moving as much as I used to.
- **That** refers to *one* thing that is *farther* away from you in space or time.
  Examples: *That* is the man who was my first sweetheart.
  I remember *that* romance like it was yesterday.
- **Those** refers to *more than one* thing that is *farther* away from you in space or time.
  Examples: *Those* are pictures of my children.
  Of course, I was younger in *those* days, too.

CHAPTER EIGHTEEN

Using Words That Tell the Action

Action words are the most important words in any language, including English. Action words are called *verbs*. Most verbs tell about an *activity*—for example, *to run, to drink, to laugh, to eat*. A few verbs tell about a *state*—for example, *to be, to seem, to remain, to sound*. Sometimes verbs need helping words (called *auxiliary words*) with them to give them a specific meaning.

ACTION WORDS: VERB TENSES

Action words can talk about what is happening (***the present***), what has happened (***the past***), and what will happen (***the future***). The *tense* of a verb is the time it talks about—present, past, or future.

The present

There are several different ways to talk about actions that happen in the present.

- You can talk about something that is happening at this *specific moment*.
- You can talk about something that happens *often*.
- You can talk about something that is *true in general*.
- You can talk about something that has been happening in the *recent past* and is *still* happening.

Something that is happening at this specific moment. There is one way to use action words to talk about something that is happening right now.

Examples: We *are listening* to the radio.
Abdul *is studying* for a test.

In this case, use the helping words **am, is,** or **are** and add **-ing** to the end of the action word.

I *am studying* — We *are studying*
You *are studying* — You *are studying*
He *is studying* — They *are studying*
She *is studying*

There is another way to talk about something that is happening right now.

Examples: We *hear* the radio.
Abdul *finishes* the book.

Something that happens often. There is only one way to use action words to talk about actions that happen often.

Examples: We *listen* to the radio every day.
Abdul *studies* all the time.

Something that is true in general. There is only one way to talk about actions that are true all the time.

Examples: We *enjoy* listening to the radio.
Abdul *believes* he will pass the test.

In these cases, there is *no change* in the action word except to talk about one other person (*he, she,* or *it*). When talking about one other person, add **-s** to the end of the action word.

Examples: I *listen* to the radio.
You *listen* to the radio.
She *listens* to the radio.

Something that has been happening in the recent past and is still happening. There is only one way to talk about something that has been happening in the recent past and is still happening.

Examples: We *have been listening* to the radio all evening.
Abdul *has been studying* hard this week.

In this case, use the helping words **have been** or **has been** and add **-ing** to the end of the action word.

I *have been studying* — We *have been studying*
You *have been studying* — You *have been studying*
He *has been studying* — They *have been studying*
She *has been studying*

The past

There are several different ways to talk about actions that happened in the past.

- You can talk about something that happened and ended in the past.
- You can talk about something that happened over a specific period of time.
- You can talk about something that happened at an unspecific time or period of time.
- You can talk about something that happened in the recent past and has ended.

Something that happened and ended in the past. There is only one way to use action words to talk about actions that happened and ended in the past.

Examples: I *washed* the dishes after dinner.
Jen *laughed* at his jokes last night.
The airplane *landed* on the runway.

To talk about actions that happened and ended in the past, add **-ed** to the action word. The word is the same whether you are talking about yourself or others, about one person or more than one.

Something that happened over a specific period of time. There is only one way to use action words to talk about actions that happened over a specific period of time.

Examples: I *was washing* the dishes when he called.
Jen *was laughing* at his jokes all evening.
The airplane *was landing* on the runway when it began to rain.

To talk about actions that happened over a specific period of time, use the helping word **was** or **were** and add **-ing** to the end of the action word.

I *was washing*
You *were washing*
He *was washing*
She *was washing*
We *were washing*
You *were washing*
They *were washing*

Something that happened at an unspecific time or period of time. There is only one way to use action words to talk about actions that happened at an unspecific time or period of time.

Examples: I *have washed* dishes all my life.
Jen *has laughed* at his jokes so hard that she pulled a muscle.
The airplane *has landed* on that runway nine hundred times.

Something that happened in the recent past and has ended.

Examples: I *have washed* the dishes already.
Jen *has laughed* a lot tonight.
The airplane *has landed* and is at the gate.

To talk about actions that happened at an unspecific time or period of time, or to talk about things that happened in the recent past and have ended, use the helping word **have** or **has** and add **-ed** to the end of the action word.

I *have washed*
You *have washed*
He *has washed*
She *has washed*
We *have washed*
You *have washed*
They *have washed*

Remember: Some action words do not follow the rules. They are different. See page 158 for a list of these different action words.

The future

There are two ways to talk about actions that will happen in the future.

- You can talk about something that will happen at a *specific* time.
- You can talk about something that will be happening over a *period* of time.

Something that will happen at a specific time. There are two ways to use action words to talk about something that will happen at a specific time. The one you choose depends upon the kind of situation you want to describe.

- *Actions* that will happen at a specific time (although the specific time may not be known). To talk about actions that will happen at a specific time, use the helping word **will** with the action word. There is no change in the action word.

Examples: I *will see* Cosimo tomorrow.
Chang *will travel* to New York City.
The store *will open* in April.

There is another way to use action words to say exactly the same thing. To talk about actions or states that will happen to yourself (*I* or *we*) or to others (*you, he, she, it,* or *they*) at a *specific* time (although the specific time may not be known), use the helping words **will be** and add **-ing** to the action word.

Examples: I *will be seeing* Cosimo tomorrow.
Chang *will be traveling* to New York City.
The store *will be opening* in April.

• *Actions* that will happen *before* other actions or states happen. To talk about actions that will happen *before* other actions happen, use the helping words **will have** and add **-ed** to the action word.

Examples: I *will have seen* Cosimo by Wednesday.
Chang *will have traveled* to New York City before I will.
The store *will have opened* by then.

Something that will be happening over a period of time. There is only one way to use action words to talk about actions that will be happening over a *period* of time: Use the helping words **will be** and add **-ing** to the action word.

Examples: I *will be seeing* Cosimo every day next week.
Chang *will be traveling* for several months.
The store *will be staying* open until the last item is sold.

ACTION WORDS: VERB FORMS

Regular Verbs

Most action words in English follow a regular pattern when they change from present to past. Here are some examples of *regular verbs:*

PRESENT	***PAST***
appear	appeared
dry	dried
enjoy	enjoyed
fix	fixed
laugh	laughed
owe	owed
plan	planned
stop	stopped
talk	talked
walk	walked

Irregular Verbs

Many common action words do not follow this regular pattern. They do not follow any rules. They change in different ways. The only way to remember how these action words change is to learn each word. The action word that is used most often in English is one example of these *irregular verbs:* **to be**: *am, are, is, was, were.* Here is a list of commonly used irregular verbs in English. Look at this list when you are not sure about how these verbs change.

PRESENT	PAST	PRESENT	PAST
awake	awoke	fly	flew
bear	bore	forbid	forbade
beat	beat	forget	forgot
become	became	forgive	forgave
begin	began	freeze	froze
bend	bent	get	got
bind	bound	give	gave
bite	bit	go	went
bleed	bled	grow	grew
blow	blew	hang	hung, hanged
break	broke	have	had
bring	brought	hear	heard
build	built	hide	hid
burst	burst	hit	hit
buy	bought	hold	held
catch	caught	hurt	hurt
choose	chose	keep	kept
come	came	know	knew
cost	cost	lead	led
cut	cut	learn	learned, learnt
deal	dealt	leave	left
dig	dug	lend	lent
do	did	let	let
draw	drew	lie	lay
drink	drank	light	lit, lighted
drive	drove	lose	lost
eat	ate	make	made
fall	fell	mean	meant
feed	fed	meet	met
feel	felt	pay	paid
fight	fought	put	put
find	found	quit	quit

PRESENT	PAST	PRESENT	PAST
read	read	steal	stole
ride	rode	stick	stuck
ring	rang	sting	stung
rise	rose	strike	struck
run	ran	swim	swam
say	said	swing	swung
see	saw	take	took
sell	sold	teach	taught
send	sent	tear	tore
shake	shook	tell	told
shine	shone	think	thought
shoot	shot	throw	threw
show	showed	understand	understood
shut	shut	upset	upset
sing	sang	wake	woke, waked
speak	spoke	wear	wore
speed	sped, speeded	win	won
spend	spent	withdraw	withdrew
spread	spread	write	wrote
stand	stood		

Action Words: Auxiliary Words

English has a number of special words that are used to *help* action words. These words are **would, can, could, shall, should, may, might,** and **must**. These helping words show four things:

- If an action or state is *able to happen.*
- If an action or state is *likely to happen.*
- If an action or state is *needed or required to happen.*
- If an action or state is *possible or all right.*

Would can help in two ways:

- Talk about something that is *possible* under certain conditions.
  Example: I *would* visit Gamesh if he were in town.
- Ask *if* something is *possible* or *likely* to happen.
  Example: *Would* you visit Gamesh with me?

Can can help in two ways:

- Talk about something that is *able to happen.*
  Example: The store *can* order shirts in your size.
- Ask *if* something is *able to happen.*
  Example: *Can* you order shirts in my size?

Note: **Can** asks if you are *able* to do something, not if you *will* do it.

Could can help in two ways:

- Talk about something that is *possible.*

Example: We *could* win the lottery.

- Ask *if* something is *possible.*

Example: *Could* we win the lottery?

Shall can help in two ways:

- Talk about something that is *likely to happen.*

Example: We *shall* never forget his kindness.

- Ask *if* something is *possible or all right.*

Example: *Shall* we go now?

Note: **Shall** is not used very often. It is formal. When used to *ask,* it is an invitation rather than a question.

Should can help in three ways:

- Talk about something that is *needed.*

Example: We *should* talk to the landlord about the leak.

- Talk about something that is *likely to happen.*

Example: The landlord *should* repair the leak tomorrow.

- Ask *if* something is *needed.*

Example: *Should* we ask the landlord to repair the leak?

May can help in two ways:

- Talk about something that is *possible.*

Example: Jesse *may* call from the hotel.

- Ask *if* something is *possible or all right.*

Example: *May* I call Jesse at the hotel?

Note: **May** and **could** are very much alike. But **may** suggests that *the person involved* can decide if the action will happen. **Could** suggests that *something else* will decide if the action will happen.

Might can help in two ways:

- Talk about something that is *possible.*

Example: We *might* find a closer parking space.

- Ask *if* something is *possible or all right.*

Example: *Might* we walk on your property?

Note: **Might** is not used often for asking questions. It is very formal. Usually **may** is used instead.

Must can help in three ways:

- Talk about something that is *needed.*

Example: You *must* talk to the doctor about that pain.

- Talk about something that is *required to happen.*

Example: You *must* finish your carrots before you can have any dessert.

- Ask *if* something is *required to happen.*

Example: *Must* I eat all my carrots?

There are also two families of action words that sometimes are used as helping words. They are action words when they are used before a *naming word* or a *describing word.* They become helping words when they are used before another *action word.*

- ***to be: am, is, are, was, were, be, being***

Examples: They *were* leaving the store.
Estela *was* kissed by a stranger.
He *is being* teased by the others.

- ***to have: has, had, have***

Examples: Someone *had* complained about her.
I *have* torn my dress.

CHAPTER NINETEEN

Using Words That Describe

English has three kinds of describing words:

- Words that describe naming words (nouns) are called *adjectives.*
- Words that describe action words (verbs) are called *adverbs.*
- Words that describe who, what, when, where, how much, or how many are also called *adverbs.*

DESCRIBING WORDS: ADJECTIVES

Describing words (adjectives) tell something about a naming word (noun). They can tell:

- What *color* it is: an *orange* moon.
- What *shape* it is: the *round* table.
- What *size* it is: the *large* dog.
- What *age* it is: the *old* house.
- *Where* it is: the *east* side.
- What its *use* is: the *carving* knife.
- What its *value* is: the *bad* apple.
- What it is *like*: the *warm* biscuit.
- How *many* there are: the *six* children.

Adjectives can be used in three places in a sentence:

- *Before* the naming word.

Examples: Hakeem bought a *red* car.
The *third* student spoke about freedom.
Her *long* braid hung down her back.

- *After* action words (verbs) that tell about a state (not an activity): *to be, to smell, to taste, to sound, to feel, to seem.*

Examples: The afternoon was *hot.*
The room smelled *stale.*
Her soup tastes *bitter.*
That cough sounds *bad.*
I felt *cold* and *clammy.*
Traffic seems *slow* today.

- *After* the describing words *very, quite, really, too,* and *so.*
  Examples: That cough sounds *very bad.*
  Traffic seems *quite slow* today.
  I felt *really cold* and clammy.
  The afternoon was *too hot.*
  Her soup tastes *so bitter.*

Describing words that show comparison (adjectives)

Adjectives can change to show ***degree*** when two or more things are being compared with each other. To show that one thing is more than another, many adjectives add **-er** and **-est** to the end of the word. If the adjective has more than two syllables, add the words **more** and **most** before the adjective. Here are some examples:

short	fast	cold	funny
short*er*	fast*er*	cold*er*	funni*er*
short*est*	fast*est*	cold*est*	funni*est*
careful	interesting	generous	likable
more careful	*more* interesting	*more* generous	*more* likable
most careful	*most* interesting	*most* generous	*most* likable

To show that one thing is less than another, add the words **less** and **least** before the adjective:

short	interesting	cold	likable
less short	*less* interesting	*less* cold	*less* likable
least short	*least* interesting	*least* cold	*least* likable

Like some action words, some degrees of adjectives do not follow a regular pattern. Here are some common examples:

good	bad	many/much	far
better	worse	more	farther/further
best	worst	most	farthest/furthest

Describing words that show how much or how many (adjectives)

Certain describing words give a general idea of *how much* or *how many* things are being described. Here is a list of these describing words:

each	every	all	some	many
much	any	few	more	less

- **Each** and **every** refer to *only one thing.*
  Examples: each house
  every school
- **All, some, many, any,** and **few** refer to *more than one thing.*
  Examples: all streets
  some women
  many men

any pillows
few books

• **All, some much, any, more,** and **less** are used with naming words that refer to a quantity of something.

Examples: all the milk
some powder
much soap
any grease
more water
less dirt

Note: Notice that **all, some,** and **any** can be used with either *quantity* naming words or *plural* naming words.

• We can also use all of these words—except **every**—without a naming word. In that case, we use them *instead of* the naming word.

Examples: Lydia added *more* cream. — Lydia added *more.*
We only saw a *few* tourists. — We only saw a *few.*

DESCRIBING WORDS: ADVERBS

Many different kinds of describing words can be used to describe action words. However, most adverbs are adjectives with **-ly** added to the end of the word. Describing words that end in **-ly** have one of these meanings:

• In a certain way (how).

Examples: The modern machine ran *quietly.*
We laughed *loudly* at the comedy show.
Sardev smiled *shyly* at her new friend.

• At a certain time (when).

Examples: I *recently* saw that film.
Mr. Chow visits her *daily.*
The club has not met *lately.*

Describing words that show comparison (adverbs)

Like adjectives, adverbs can change to show ***degree*** when two or more actions are being compared with each other. To show that one thing is more than another, many adverbs add **-er** and **-est** to the end of the word. Others add the words **more** and **most**.

near	slow	early	friendly
near*er*	slow*er*	earli*er*	friendli*er*
near*est*	slow*est*	earli*est*	friendli*est*
fully	suddenly	deeply	smoothly
more fully	*more* suddenly	*more* deeply	*more* smoothly
most fully	*most* suddenly	*most* deeply	*most* smoothly

To show that one thing is less than another, add the words **less** and **least** before the adverb.

near	suddenly	early	smoothly
less near	*less* suddenly	*less* early	*less* smoothly
least near	*least* suddenly	*least* early	*least* smoothly

Like some action words and some adjectives, some degrees of adverbs do not follow a regular pattern. Here are some common examples:

well	badly	little	far
better	worse	less	farther/further
best	worst	least	farthest/furthest

Describing words that show when, where, how far, and how often (adverbs)

Certain describing words show when, where, how far, and how often an action happens. Here is a list of these describing words:

now	in	here	once
then	out	there	twice
soon	up	far	always
still	down	near	never
first	over		
last	under		
	inside		
	outside		
	by		
	on		

- **Now, then, soon, still, first,** and **last** describe *when* an action happens.

  Examples: She is calling *now.*
  Then Juan remembered her.
  I *still* enjoy loud music.
  They were seated *first.*
  Russell arrived *last.*

- **In, out, up, down, over, under, inside, outside, by,** and **on** show *where* an action happens.

  Examples: She ran *in* and *out.*
  The elevator goes *up* and *down.*
  I ran *over* a snake.
  Chou hid *under* the bed.
  He was locked *inside* the store.
  The children looked *outside.*
  I drove *by* the store.
  Elsa was cut *on* her knee.

- **Here, there, far,** and **near** show *how far* away an action happens.

  Examples: My keys were *here* yesterday.
  The couch goes *there.*
  They searched *far* and *near.*

- **Once, twice, always,** and **never** show *how often* an action happens.

  Examples: She trotted *once* around the track.
  He has missed class *twice.*
  It *always* snows in January.
  Mimi *never* smiles.

CHAPTER TWENTY

Using Words That Connect

English has two kinds of connecting words:

- Words that show how people, places, things, or actions are connected in *time* and *space* are called ***prepositions.*** For example: Mary arrived *after* Frank (time). She sat *beside* Fred (space).
- Words that show how people, places, things, or actions are connected in other ways (similarities/differences, cause/effect, etc.) are called ***conjunctions.*** For example: She sang loud *but* off-key (similarities/differences). She sang off-key *because* she had a cold (cause/effect).

CONNECTING WORDS: PREPOSITIONS

Showing a time connection

Some connecting words help you talk about time. They tell *when* something happens, has happened, or will happen.

Connecting words that show time

now	then	soon	still
first	last	always	never
after	before	during	until
since	often	rarely	finally
also	already	yet	hardly ever
afterwards	while	once	as
ever	ever since	as long as	as soon as

Sometimes these words come at the beginning of a sentence.

Examples: *Now* we are ready for a little dessert!
Then we can sit and talk in front of the fire.
After Magda had her operation, she started knitting.
Before we go to the store, let's make a shopping list.
Until the puppy stops chewing things, she must be kept outdoors.
During October, we plan to clean the garage.
As the years go by, you look younger and younger.
Soon I will take my citizenship test.
Afterwards, we plan to see a movie.
While the weather is warm, let's leave the windows open.

Sometimes these words come in the middle of a sentence.

Examples: Lina cannot come home *until* the semester is over.
We have been best friends *since* the third grade.
Jesse *always* wanted a motorcycle.
I hope we can *finally* settle this problem!
My parents will help out *as long as* we need them to.
Can you come by *after* the lunch today?
José and Socorro had fun *during* the party.
I never know *when* the furnace will work.
Although we see each other *often*, we aren't really friends.
I want to speak with her *as soon as* she gets here.

Showing a space connection

Some connecting words tell where to find something. These location words tell where one thing is located in relation to another.

Connecting words that show location

near	far	next to	between
behind	in front of	across from	above
below	around	beside	outside of
inside of	under	here	there

Sometimes these words come at the beginning of a sentence.

Examples: *Across from* the courthouse you will see the jail.
Inside of the cabinet is where I keep my dishes.
Between my house and my nearest neighbor is a ditch
Below his name, his dates of birth and death are given.

Sometimes these words come in the middle of a sentence.

Examples: The electrical outlet is *behind* the couch.
Trim the bush that is *near* the driveway.
Everyone got *here* just in time for dinner.
The sugar jar sits *beside* the flour jar.

CONNECTING WORDS: CONJUNCTIONS

Words that join "two of a kind"

Connecting words that join two of a kind are called ***coordinating conjunctions.*** "Two of a kind" means two naming words, two action words, two describing words, and even two sentences or parts of sentences. Here is a list of coordinating conjunctions:

and or yet but

- Use the word **and** to show *addition.*
  Examples: Mary *and* Joe called to say hello.
  It was raining cats *and* dogs!
- Use the word **or** to show *alternation.*
  Examples: Do you want chocolate *or* vanilla?
  I will wear either red *or* brown.
- Use the words **but** and **yet** to show *opposition.*
  Examples: I want to rest, *but* I must work.
  She is skinny *but* muscular.
  He was a stern man, *yet* he was kind.

Words that show comparison

When you're comparing two things, you will often need to use connecting words that show this kind of relationship. These words are called ***comparative conjunctions.*** Here are pairs of connecting words that compare:

more . . . than
less . . . than
as . . . as
so . . . that

These are examples of comparative conjunctions in sentences:

Examples: My uncle is *more* generous *than* my aunt.
No country offers *more* opportunity *than* America.
Lin-Lin is *as* smart *as* a computer!
No one plays chess *as* well *as* Nicholas.
The weather is *so* hot *that* you can fry an egg on the sidewalk!
Mano speaks English *so* well *that* he got a job as a translator.

Words that show different relationships

Some connecting words are used to join *two sentences*, making them into *one sentence with two related ideas*. These connecting words are called ***subordinating conjunctions*** and ***conjunctive adverbs***. Here are some common connecting words of this type:

although	even though	even if	if
because	since	so	unless
while	so that	that	

Examples: We stopped at the accident *because* we thought we could help.
Nu wrote them a letter *so* they could understand his wishes.
I won't go to work, *since* I am feeling bad.
Marcus wants to go, *while* Marcie wants to stay.
He doesn't like her, *although* she has done nothing to hurt him.

These connecting words connect two parts of a sentence together and at the same time show how those two parts are related to each other. The connecting words can show *contrast, cause and effect,* and *possibility.*

• When you want to show how two things are not alike, you use connecting words that show *contrast.*

Examples: We will mail the package, *although* we doubt she will receive it.
Our uncle insists on buying a house, *even though* he has no money to pay for it.
I have decided to get my college degree, *even if* it takes me twenty years.

• When you want to show how one thing affects another thing, you use connecting words that show *cause and effect.*

Examples: Imad made an A in the course *because* he studied hard.
They cannot take Accounting II *since* they have not taken Accounting I.
We baked lots of cookies *so that* we wouldn't run out.

• When you want to show how one thing *might* affect another thing, you use connecting words that show *possibility.*

Examples: *If* my brother comes to visit, I will make a traditional feast in his honor.
Olga cannot join us this evening, *unless* her mother comes home earlier than expected.

Usually, the word **that** follows words like **except, in,** and **so** to make a subordinating conjunction. However, the word **that** may be used alone after these special action words:

Special action words coming before "that"

say	believe	think	decide	see/hear
agree	propose	prove	suggest	assume
demand	wish	hope	confess	recommend

Examples: He said *that* he wanted turkey for dinner.
Bob thinks *that* Melinda likes him.
May I suggest *that* everyone be quiet?
I hear *that* you are engaged.
Papa demanded *that* we tell him where we had been.

Words that show a transition

Some connecting words help you move from one thought to another.

Words that show transition

as a result	for example	in fact
in other words	as well as	after all
finally	eventually	as a result
otherwise	next	however
also	besides	

Sometimes these connecting words help to further explain something you have already been talking about.

Examples: James is losing his house *as a result* of being laid off from his job.
In fact, he was a hard worker and should not have been fired.

Sometimes these words let your audience know you are about to conclude or give a sense of time to your description.

Examples: *Finally,* we must study this matter carefully.
If we take our time, we may *eventually* arrive at a good solution.

CHAPTER TWENTY-ONE

Using Different Kinds of Sentences

In English, there are three basic kinds of sentences:

- Telling sentences.
- Asking sentences.
- Command sentences.

TELLING SENTENCES

The most commonly used sentences are telling sentences. These sentences follow this basic pattern: naming word + action word. For example: *I laughed. I* is a substitute naming word and *laughed* is an action word.

However, most telling sentences are not this simple. Usually they have connecting words and describing words as well. There may be more than one naming word, more than one action word, an action word phrase, or describing words. Here are some examples:

Morris and *Nook* are brothers. (more than one naming word)
I *got up* and *got dressed.* (more than one action word)
Morris *went to the store.* (action word phrase)
The red balloon popped *loudly.* (describing word)

Connecting words can also be used to join short sentences together:

Henry likes his new job, but *he does not like his boss.*
The teacher graded papers until *she fell asleep.*

ASKING SENTENCES

Asking sentences are called *questions*. Questions begin in two ways:

- With an *action word* or *helping word*. These questions can be answered with "yes" or "no."
  Examples: *Will* you call me tomorrow? *Yes.*
  Did you buy a new suit? *No.*

- With an *asking word.* These questions must be answered with a new fact.
  Examples: *How* are you feeling? *My headache is better.*
  When will they get here? *Next week.*

Using helping or action words

Here are a few common helping or action words you will use often to ask questions.

to be: am, is, are, was, were, will be	*Am* I on time?
	Is she here?
	Are they hungry?
	Was the shop closed?
	Were the children sick?
	Will you *be* here tomorrow?
to do: do, does, did, will do	*Do* you know my neighbor?
	Does she have a car?
	Did you get the milk?
	Will the plumber *do* the job?
to have: has, have, will have	*Has* her sister left yet?
	Have we heard from Angie?
	Will you *have* your hair cut?

Here are the two ways you can build questions that begin with an action word or a helping word:

- Action word + naming word + action word
  Did *she* *clean?*

- Action word + naming word + naming or describing word
  Is *Manuel* *a teacher?*

Using asking words

Here are the seven asking words to use when asking a question:

- who *Who* is at the door?
- when *When* did you see her?
- where *Where* are my new shoes?
- why *Why* did he drive away so fast?
- what *What* kind of soap do you use?
- how *How* do you clean grease spots?
- which *Which* one of you broke the glass?

COMMAND SENTENCES

When you tell or ask someone to do something, you use a command sentence. This type of sentence usually begins with an action word. The person who is being told or asked to do the action is not mentioned. The person understands that he or she is being asked or told to do something.

Examples: *Get* some apples and pears.
Sweep the kitchen and bathroom.
Tell me what happened.

Command sentences are sometimes used to give orders. Other times they are used to make requests. Use the word *please* to show that you are making a request instead of giving an order.

APPENDIX A

APPENDIX A

Pronunciation Guidelines

Adding sounds to the end of a word

There are two situations in which you add the sound of **-s, -z,** or **-ez** to the end of the word.

- *With naming words:* when you speak of more than one person, place, or thing.
- *With action words:* when you talk about something that is happening in the present to one person, place, or thing. ***Note:*** *Not* when speaking of yourself (***I***) or speaking to someone else (***you***).

Here are some guidelines to tell which sound you should use. *Add the* ***-s*** *sound to:*

- Words ending with the sound of **k**.
  For example: *leaks, spanks, parks.*
- Words ending with the sound of **p**.
  For example: *lips, crops, drips.*
- Words ending with the sound of **t**.
  For example: *dots, carpets, plates.*
- *Most* words ending with the sound of **f**.
  For example: *beliefs, proofs, coughs.*

However, there are *some* words ending with the sound of **f** that change to the sound of **vz**: *thief* changes to *thieves, scarf* changes to *scarves, leaf* changes to *leaves, knife* changes to *knives, life* changes to *lives, shelf* changes to *shelves, calf* changes to *calves, loaf* changes to *loaves*. *Add the -z sound to:*

- Words ending with the sound of **a, i, o, oo, ow,** or **oi**.
  For example: *bananas, seas, skies, heroes, canoes, cows, boys.*
- Words ending with the sound of **b**.
  For example: *cribs, mobs, grabs.*
- Words ending with the sound of **d**.
  For example: *suds, ends, stands.*
- Words ending with the sound of **g**.
  For example: *frogs, drugs, catalogues.*
- Words ending with the sound of **m**.
  For example: *hymns, crams, comes.*
- Words ending with the sound of **n**.
  For example: *conditions, lines, tons.*
- Words ending with the sound of **ng**.
  For example: *songs, rungs, tongues.*

- Words ending with the sound of **r**.
  For example: *robbers, pears, liars.*
- Words ending with the sound of **v**.
  For example: *valves, carves, drives.*

Add the ***-ez*** *sound to:*

- Words ending with the sound of **j**.
  For example: *charges, judges, badges.*
- Words ending with the sound of **s**.
  For example: *kisses, laces, prices.*
- Words ending with the sound of **sh**.
  For example: *crashes, wishes, squashes.*
- Words ending with the sound of **ch**.
  For example: *lunches, watches, bunches.*
- Words ending with the sound of **x** or **z**.
  For example: *taxes, buzzes.*

Joining two words

In English, certain words can be shortened and then joined to other words. These two joined words together are called a *contraction.* The words that can be shortened are: *will, have,* and *not.*

Here are some examples:

Two words	*Contraction*
I will	I'll
they will	they'll
Dad will	Dad'll (not common)
could have	could've (not common)
will not	won't
do not	don't

Shortening words

In English, sometimes people cut off parts of words. The shorter piece of the word that they speak is called an *abbreviation.* Here are some examples of words that people often abbreviate:

Complete word	***Abbreviation***
automobile	auto
airplane	plane
telephone	phone
refrigerator	fridge
shopping mall	mall
television	TV
videocassette recorder	VCR
health maintenance organization	HMO

Using words that sound alike but mean different things

English has a number of words that sound alike but have different meanings. They usually are spelled differently, too, though not always. If you know the meaning of only *one* of these sound-alike words, you might get confused when a person uses the sound-alike word with a different meaning. Here is a short list of sound-alike words that you may hear. Notice the differences in types of words and in meanings.

accept	(action word) to take what is offered
except	(connecting word) but
allowed	(action word) to allow in the past
aloud	(describing word) using the voice
altar	(naming word) a table used for worship
alter	(action word) to change
bare	(describing word) without covering
bear	(naming word) large animal
board	(naming word) a long, flat piece of wood
bored	(describing word) feeling dull and tired
brake	(naming word) something that slows or stops
break	(action word) to split into pieces
by	(describing word) next to, beside
buy	(action word) to pay money for
coarse	(describing word) rough
course	(naming word) a school program of study
die	(action word) to stop living
dye	(action word) to color
dye	(naming word) something used to color

do (action word) to act
due (describing word) expected or scheduled

hear (action word) to take in by ear
here (describing word) at this place or time

heard (action word) to take in by ear in the past
herd (naming word) a group of animals, a crowd

knead (action word) to press or squeeze
need (action word) to want, to require

knot (naming word) a fastening
not (describing word) no

lead (naming word) a heavy metal
led (action word) to lead in the past

left (action word) to leave in the past
left (describing word) the side opposite the right side

lie (action word) to tell an untruth
lie (action word) to rest upon something else

mean (action word) to intend
mean (describing word) bad-tempered

meat (naming word) flesh of an animal
meet (action word) to come together

pail (naming word) bucket
pale (describing word) white, colorless

pain (naming word) hurt
pane (naming word) a piece of glass in a window

pair (naming word) two
pear (naming word) a fruit
pare (action word) to take off the skin

patient (naming word) a person who is taken care of by a doctor
patient (describing word) not giving up or getting angry

peace (naming word) no war or anger
piece (naming word) a portion

pedal (naming word) a bar worked by the foot
petal (naming word) a piece of a flower

pen (naming word) a cage
pen (naming word) something to write with

plane (naming word) airplane
plain (describing word) simple; not fancy

pole (naming word) a long shaft of wood or metal
pole (naming word) one of two opposite points
poll (naming word) a survey of public opinion

present (naming word) being someplace
present (naming word) gift

right (describing word) opposite of left
right (describing word) correct
right (naming word) something due by law or tradition
write (action word) to put into letters and words

ring (action word) to make a bell sound
ring (naming word) jewelry for the finger

road (naming word) a path for cars, bicycles, etc.
rode (action word) to ride in the past

role (naming word) a part someone acts
roll (naming word) a small bread

sail (action word) to travel by boat
sale (naming word) an event when prices are lowered in a store

saw (action word) to have seen in the past
saw (naming word) a tool for cutting

so (describing word) very much; very clear
sew (action word) to stitch

tail (naming word) the rear end
tale (naming word) a story

threw (action word) to throw in the past
through (describing word) from one end to the other

to (connecting word) in a direction toward
too (describing word) more than enough
two (naming word) the number after one

waist (naming word) the middle of the body
waste (naming word) garbage, trash
waste (action word) to use carelessly

way (naming word) course or direction
weigh (action word) to measure heaviness

wait (action word) to stay in one place
weight (naming word) heaviness

weak (describing word) without strength or energy
week (naming word) seven days

Speaking too fast

People sometimes speak so quickly that they do not pronounce the words correctly. Usually, they combine several words together and change the final sounds. Here are some common examples. If you hear these words, you can look at this list to figure out what they mean.

Sounds like	***Means***
gonna	going to
wanna	want to
hafta	have to
dunno	don't know
lemme	let me
gimme	give me or give it to me
coulda or coulduv	could have
couldenuv	couldn't have
woulda or woulduv	would have
wouldenuv	wouldn't have
shoulda or shoulduv	should have
shouldenuv	shouldn't have
whatta	what do

People also cut off the last letter of words ending in **-ing** when they speak too fast. Here are a few examples:

bein	being	givin	giving
goin	going	doin	doing
havin	having	lookin	looking

APPENDIX B

APPENDIX B

Numbers and Measurements

Numbers

There are two ways to express numbers. *Cardinal* numbers express amount or value. *Ordinal* numbers express order or sequence.

Examples: Juana has *two* children
(cardinal: the *number* of children she has)
Juana's *second* child is a boy.
(ordinal: the *order* in which her children were born)

Say and write cardinal and ordinal numbers like this:

CARDINAL NUMBERS		***ORDINAL NUMBERS***	
1	one	lst	first
2	two	2nd	second
3	three	3rd	third
4	four	4th	fourth
5	five	5th	fifth
6	six	6th	sixth
7	seven	7th	seventh
8	eight	8th	eighth
9	nine	9th	ninth
10	ten	10th	tenth
11	eleven	11th	eleventh
12	twelve	12th	twelfth
13	thirteen	13th	thirteenth
14	fourteen	14th	fourteenth
15	fifteen	15th	fifteenth
16	sixteen	16th	sixteenth
17	seventeen	17th	seventeenth
18	eighteen	18th	eighteenth
19	nineteen	19th	nineteenth
20	twenty	20th	twentieth
21	twenty-one	21st	twenty-first
22	twenty-two	22nd	twenty-second
23	twenty-three	23rd	twenty-third
24	twenty-four	24th	twenty-fourth
25	twenty-five	25th	twenty-fifth
30	thirty	30th	thirtieth
40	forty	40th	fortieth
50	fifty	50th	fiftieth
60	sixty	60th	sixtieth
70	seventy	70th	seventieth
80	eighty	80th	eightieth
90	ninety	90th	ninetieth
100	one hundred	100th	one hundredth

Note: Fractions are pronounced as a combination of cardinal and ordinal numbers. For example, the fraction *4/5* would be called *four-fifths*. Some commonly used fractions have special names:

1/2 is called *one-half*

1/4 can be called *one-quarter* as well as *one-fourth*

3/4 can be called *three-quarters* as well as *three-fourths*.

Measurements: American and Metric Systems

Here is a chart showing equivalent measurements of *length, area, volume/capacity,* and *weight* in the Metric System and the American System.

	American	Metric	Metric	American
Length				
	1 inch (1")	2.54 centimeters	1 centimeter	0.394 inch
	1 foot (1')	0.305 meter	1 decimeter	3.937 inches
	1 yard	0.914 meter	1 meter	39.37 inches
	1 mile	1.609 kilometers	1 kilometer	0.621 mile
Area				
	1 square inch	6.452 sq. cm.	1 square cm.	0.155 sq. in.
	1 square foot	929.030 sq. cm.		
	1 square yard	0.836 sq. m.	1 centare	10.764 sq. ft.
	1 acre	4,047 sq. m.	1 hectare	2.477 acres
Volume/Capacity				
	1 pint	0.473 liter	1 deciliter	0.211 pint
	1 quart	0.946 liter	1 liter	1.057 quarts
	1 gallon	3.785 liters	1 decaliter	2.642 gallons
Weight				
	1 ounce	28.350 grams	1 decagram	0.353 ounce
	1 pound	453.592 grams	1 kilogram	2.205 pounds
	1 ton	0.907 metric ton	1 metric ton	1.102 tons

Measurements: American System equivalents

Here are equivalent measurements within the American System.

MEASUREMENT	EQUIVALENT
1 foot	12 inches
1 yard	3 feet, 36 inches
1 mile	1,760 yards, 5,280 feet
1 square foot	144 square inches
1 square yard	9 square feet, 1,296 square inches
1 acre	4,840 square yards, 43,560 square feet
1 square mile	640 acres
1 tablespoon	3 teaspoons, 1/2 fluid ounce
1 cup	16 tablespoons, 8 fluid ounces, 1/2 pint
1 pint	16 fluid ounces, 2 cups
1 quart	2 pints, 32 fluid ounces
1 gallon	4 quarts, 128 fluid ounces
1 pound	16 ounces
1 ton	2,000 pounds

Measurements: Fahrenheit and Celsius

Here is a chart showing equivalents between the Fahrenheit and Celsius methods of measuring temperature.

	FAHRENHEIT	*CELSIUS*
Freezing point of water	32°	0°
Cool day	50°	10°
Warm day	86°	30°
Normal body temperature	98.6°	37°
Heat-wave conditions	104°	40°

ANSWER KEY

Exercise Answer Key

Exercise 1.1
1. How many bedrooms do Ping and Laura need in their apartment?
2. When will the town house be available?
3. What does the kitchen have?
4. Which house is the most expensive?
5. How will Juana drive to work?
6. Why does the landlord want a pet deposit?
7. When will you give us/me the key?
8. Where are the washer and dryer connections?
9. Who must water and mow the yard?
10. Which parking space can we use?

Exercise 1.2
1. at this specific moment
2. in general
3. at this specific moment
4. at this specific moment
5. often
6. in general
7. at this specific moment
8. in general
9. at this specific moment

Exercise 1.3
1. are looking
2. want
3. need
4. want
5. visits
6. stays
7. understand
8. think
9. cost
10. drive
11. are talking
12. am looking

Exercise 2.1
1. E
2. E or R
3. U or R
4. E
5. U
6. S
7. U
8. S
9. E

Exercise 2.2

1. started
2. cashed
3. sold
4. have done
5. handled
6. was working
7. started
8. took
9. graduated
10. have studied
11. completed

Exercise 2.3

1. my interview
2. my hands
3. my application, my experience
4. my job
5. mine
6. my favorite job
7. my father
8. my fear

Exercise 3.1

1. Nasir and Tama will open a checking account.
2. They will live at the River Plaza Apartments.
3. Nasir and Tama will have an ATM number.
4. Nasir and Tama will put $200 in their checking account.
5. Vanessa will type up several papers and the Kashems will sign them.
6. Tama will deposit two checks in her account.
7. Tama will want to write a check for cash.
8. Tama will have her account debited for the traveler's checks.
9. Nasir and Tama will open a savings account.
10. Tama will go back to the bank alone.

Exercise 3.2

1. put
2. go, get
3. buy
4. give
5. put
6. hand
7. give
8. stop, pick up, let

Exercise 3.3

1. these
2. this
3. this, that
4. this
5. that
6. that
7. this
8. that
9. these
10. this

Exercise 4.1

1. O
2. O
3. O
4. M
5. O
6. M
7. M
8. O
9. M
10. O
11. M
12. O
13. M
14. O
15. O

Exercise 4.2

1. I bought many.
2. I used some.
3. I drank more.
4. Li chose many.
5. Li bought one of each.
6. I don't have any.
7. I don't need much.
8. There isn't any.
9. I need less for the bread.
10. I need more for the cake.

Exercise 5.1

1. Can you take this package to the post office tomorrow?
2. Can you send it to my mother?
3. Would I give you the address if I knew it?
4. Could he help me if he had time?
5. Can we find the post office?

6. Could we find the post office if we had a map?
7. May I have the envelope?
8. Would I mail the letter if I had time?
9. Could she pick up the mail, if she isn't too busy?
10. May he buy insurance for the package?

Exercise 5.2
1. he
2. him
3. she
4. him
5. he
6. him
7. her
8. he
9. she
10. her

Exercise 5.3
1. her
2. his
3. its
4. its
5. her
6. its
7. her
8. its
9. its
10. its
11. mother's
12. father's
13. boy's
14. letter's
15. clerk's

Exercise 6.1
1. we
2. us
3. they
4. us and them
5. us
6. we
7. them
8. they
9. we and they
10. we

Exercise 6.2
1. ours
2. their
3. our
4. our
5. their
6. ours
7. our
8. their
9. theirs
10. ours

Exercise 6.3
1. feel, am, was, will be
2. is, was, will be, feels, seems
3. is, was, will be, smells, tastes
4. is, was, will be, feels, seems
5. is, was, will be, seems
6. is, was, will be, seems
7. is, was, will be
8. are, were, will be
9. is, was
10. is, was, will be, feels, seems

Exercise 7.1
1. He is feeling bad. He's feeling bad.
2. I am wishing we could talk. I'm wishing we could talk.
3. You are thinking of her. You're thinking of her.
4. We are hoping he will return. We're hoping he'll return.
5. José is talking to her. José's talking to her.

Exercise 7.2
1. I hope he will come.
2. She will carry big boxes.
3. Socorro will wait for his call.
4. José will wish he'd called.
5. Estela will want the tables.
6. Lisa and Estela will work together.
7. Socorro and José will like each other.
8. José will call Socorro.

Exercise 7.3
1. finally, already
2. often, rarely, still, also, always, never

3. first, always, still, finally
4. now, then, also, already, never, finally
5. before, after, during, until
6. now, afterwards, soon, finally
7. first, then, already, soon, finally

Exercise 8.1

1. parking
2. right
3. beautiful
4. sunny
5. hiking
6. shady, cool
7. good, national
8. very crowded
9. beautiful
10. granite, very impressive

Exercise 8.2

1. wonderful, crowded, interesting
2. huge, tall
3. beautiful, crowded, green, huge, busy, wonderful, noisy
4. beautiful, crowded, busy, wonderful, noisy
5. beautiful, warm, crowded, busy
6. beautiful, happy, wonderful, noisy . . . warm, green, soft, tall
7. interesting, busy, wonderful
8. warm, crowded, busy, noisy
9. beautiful, huge, soft
10. crowded, interesting, noisy

Exercise 8.3

1. between
2. near, behind, in front of, next to, across from, beside, outside of, inside of
3. near, around
4. far
5. near, behind, in front of, next to, across from, beside
6. near, below, in front of, under
7. near, around, beside
8. around
9. near, in front of, behind, across from, next to, outside of
10. near, behind, in front of, across from, outside of, inside of

Exercise 9.1

1. Did Su Li visit the doctor?
2. Does Su Li's daughter need medicine?
3. Do you have the form with you?
4. Is the doctor ready to see me?
5. Has she finished the checkup?
6. Do you have questions for the doctor?
7. Was the doctor in?
8. Have you taken your medicine?
9. Is she taking medicine?
10. Are they here to see the doctor?

Exercise 9.2

1. H, gladly
2. H, quickly
3. H, thoroughly
4. H, confidently
5. H, gently
6. H, slightly
7. H, calmly
8. W, daily
9. W, immediately
10. W, gradually

Exercise 10.1

1. after
2. when
3. after
4. as soon as
5. ever since
6. once
7. as long as
8. whenever
9. before
10. until

Exercise 11.1

1. W
2. O
3. O
4. W
5. O
6. O
7. O
8. O
9. W
10. O
11. W

Exercise 11.2
1. proposed
2. decided, agreed
3. says, thinks, believes
4. said, agreed, thought, decided, suggested, recommended
5. said, wished
6. said

Exercise 11.3
1. someone
2. both
3. everyone, everybody, anyone, anybody
4. none
5. someone, somebody
6. something
7. something, everything
8. everyone, everybody
9. someone, somebody, anyone, anybody
10. nothing

Exercise 12.1
1. PSW
2. FB
3. PC
4. PC
5. FW
6. PSB
7. FW
8. PSB
9. FB

Exercise 12.2
1. were attending
2. had been studying
3. was taking
4. had been wondering
5. had heard
6. was just thinking
7. will have completed
8. will have been studying
9. will have rested

Exercise 12.3
1. because
2. although, even though, even if
3. unless, although, even though, even if
4. because, since
5. unless
6. although, even though
7. because, since, although, even though
8. if, since, because
9. even if
10. because, since

Exercise 13.1
1. cleaner, cleanest
2. easier
3. better, best
4. worse, worst
5. less, least

Exercise 13.2
1. more, than
2. so, that
3. as, as . . . less, than
4. more, than
5. so, that
6. so, that
7. more, than

Exercise 14.1
1. herself
2. myself
3. yourself
4. herself
5. itself
6. yourself
7. ourselves
8. themselves
9. himself
10. myself

Exercise 14.2
1. whose, mothers were working
2. who, worked in her office
3. which, Tran liked to play
4. who, needed a secretary
5. which, was in the Philippines
6. whose, mind is working right
7. which, she loved to eat
8. whose, life has not been easy
9. who, is talking to Tran
10. which, has a population

Exercise 15.1
1. seeing
2. planning, taking
3. going
4. developing
5. packing

Exercise 15.2
1. to ride all night in the bus
Riding all night in the bus is the way to get an early start.
2. lying in the sun on a tropical beach
To lie in the sun on a tropical beach is my idea of a great vacation.
3. listening to calypso music
To listen to calypso music reminds me of my trip to Jamaica.
4. to see the Matterhorn
Seeing the Matterhorn would be fun!
5. sleeping in my hammock
To sleep in my hammock is how I want to spend my vacation.

Exercise 15.3
1. if
2. okay
3. if
4. okay
5. as if, as though
6. if
7. okay
8. okay

Exercise 16.1
1. They must fix the toilet before the weekend.
2. We must stay in the shelter until we find jobs.
3. The garbage must be picked up.
4. My neighbor must be told that his dog must be on a leash.
5. We must know what to do right away.
6. We must not let people drive too fast on this street.
7. The city must not let these tree branches damage the electric lines.
8. I must have the stop sign put up so my children can play safely.
9. You must call a legal-aid society for help with that crooked loan company.
10. We must not put up with this trouble.

Exercise 16.2
1. after all
2. eventually
3. instead
4. otherwise
5. in other words
6. however
7. as well as
8. next
9. after all